OPEN A NEW DOOR

BY: Conrad George

DeVorss & Co.
Box 550
Marina del Rey,
Calif. 90291

9/95

Illustrations by: MIKE COLLARD

FIRST PRINTING - 1979

ISBN: 0-87516-374-2

Bookstore

"WITHOUT FRICTION
THERE IS NO
GROWTH!!"

DEDICATION

THIS BOOK IS LOVINGLY DEDICATED TO ALL
OF MY TEACHERS (even though some of
them didn't know that they were my
teachers). THEIR HELP, UNDERSTANDING,
AND PATIENCE IS GRATEFULLY ACKNOWLEDGED.

D.R.C.A.	-	E.C.	-	C.P.
L.B.W.	-	L.T.Y.	-	L.T.Z.R.
G.L.S.	-	R.E.D.	-	S.M.
R.D.	-	S.R.	-	E.D.P.
	-	R.T.J.N.	-	

CONTENTS

INTRODUCTION

WHO OR WHAT IS GOD? WHAT IS DEATH? WHAT IS
LOVE? WHY WAS I BORN?

How many times have you asked these questions or
you've heard someone else ask them? I know that
I've asked them many times. I've searched for
the answers in many religions and in many books.
I've listened to many great teachers and followed
what they taught. But, somehow, I never felt
that the answers they were teaching were 100%
true for me. There was always a gap or some
question left unanswered, and the things they did
teach would somehow just miss the mark. Their
teachings did help me a great deal in my quest
for the truth, and their answers to many of my
questions did seem correct, but where was the
proof? How could I know for sure?

I then came to the conclusion that much of this
knowledge must come from within me. It could
never be completely proven by scientific methods.
(Although many of my questions have been answered
by science and I believe many more soon will be).
If I were to truly know these answers, I would
have to proceed in a scientific way. So I've
brought the questions that have bothered me the
most, out into the open. I've studied them indi-
vidually and compared them against all the things
that I have learned in the past. I've looked at
them together to see if some of these questions
are really a part of other questions, or have
been answered by other questions. I've tried to
be as scientific as possible so that I could have
a clear understanding in my quest for the truth.
I knew that if I could come to a logical conclusion on any question, then I must have the answer
or be close to it. (And in this subject, logic
doesn't always work). Therefore, logic had to
play a big part in my approach.

The Table of Contents of this book, represent a
few of my many questions. I have written them
down and given my answers here only because I
believe that there must be others, like me, seeking answers to these same questions. Maybe the
answers that I have discovered will help answer
your questions, or will cause you to think, and
to find your own answers.

Over the years, I have discovered that my thinking changes from time to time. Things that I
learned last year and felt were true for me then
I now think differently about. And some of the
things that I did not accept last year, I now
accept. So, I have learned that my mind and my
thinking changes just as truth can change. It's
just like the old joke in the Economics Class,
"From year to year they never change the questions on the exams, they just change the answers".
And so it goes with life.

Life is really made up of change, and this change
is also in our thinking. I know that when I read
this book five years from now, my thinking will
be completely different from what it is today,
and I know that some of the answers that I believe today, I will not agree with then.

Many things today in the psychic world are unexplained. Our scientists have found no proof of
existence of higher planes of consciousness.
However, we must always keep our minds open to
new things and to new changes, because we never
know what the future will bring in scientific
discoveries. (They use to think that the Earth
was flat.)

The following excerpt is from a Boston newspaper,
bearing a Mid-19th Centry dateline and illus-
trates how our scientific values change:

"A man about 46 years of age, giving the name of
Joshua Coppersmith has been arrested in New York
for attempting to extort funds from ignorant and
superstitious people, by exhibiting a device
which, he says, will convey the human voice any
distance, over metallic wires, so that it will be
heard by the listener at the other end. He calls
the instrument a TELEPHONE, which is obviously
intended to imitate the word Telegraph and win
the confidence of those who know the success of
the latter instrument, without understanding the
principle on which it is based. Well informed
people know that it is impossible to transmit
the human voice over wires as may be done with
dots and dashes of the Morse Code and that were
it possible to do so, the thing would be of no
practical value. The authorities who apprehended
this criminal are to be congratulated, and it is
hoped that his punishment will be prompt and fit-
ting and that it may serve as an example to other
consciousless schemers who enrich themselves at
the expense of their fellow creatures."

It is obvious that back then new things and
changes were not widely accepted. So please,
dear readers, keep your minds open and receptive
to change. Change always will be, THERE IS
NOTHING PERMANENT EXCEPT CHANGE ITSELF ! ! !

WHO AND WHAT IS GOD ?

How many times have you heard someone say, "GOD
is everything," or "GOD is watching over us", or
"GOD has counted every bird in the sky" ? Although these sayings do make sense, they still
don't answer our question of who and what is GOD.
Maybe it would be better if we decided what GOD
isn't. GOD isn't the old man with the long
beard sitting on a marble throne who passes
judgement on sinners and hands down favors to
the righteous. GOD must be much more than that.
But what are his limits, if he has any, and is he
male or female?

I don't know how to prove what I feel GOD is, but
I do feel that GOD is limitless. HE has no
bounds and there is nothing to limit him. GOD is
neither male nor female. HE is both positive and
negative and is everything and no-thing.

I could find no scientific proof of the theory
that I am about to explain, it is just a composit
of all that I have been taught.

Science has discovered that there are many types
of radio waves in the air around us. They don't
know what the purpose is of many of these waves,
or where they come from. They just know that
there is something there that they can't explain.

GOD is this current, these unexplained radio
waves that flow in space through all things,
planets and beings, giving them their life and
their form. I like to refer to it as the GOD
FORCE. This GOD FORCE is everything and yet nothing, it is intelligent and yet not intelligent,
like electricity or water. It is a life force,
giving life to everything. It is energy, light,
vibration, radio waves, temperature, invisible
forces, matter, atoms and everything ever thought

of, but yet no one thing.

This GOD FORCE is a part of all things. But yet
it cares not for anything. It flows like the
river just following its natural course, following its own LAWS. The GOD FORCE is like a current flowing in space, making eddys, rapids or
smooth areas from atoms, electricity, light, and
vibration, but most important of all, the GOD
FORCE is LAW. The GOD FORCE is everything and yet
is no-thing, no-thing that you can point to and
say "That is GOD !" This GOD FORCE is an energy
field around all of us and is like the radio waves
only much more, in that it gives us our life and
our being. It is in every atom in the universe,
and is in every atom in our sub-universe.

Science has shown us that there is an electrical
field around everything, and that there is electricity in the earth and in the air itself.
Everytime we comb our hair we demonstrate this
principle by creating static electricity. The
radio waves are in the air all around us all the
time. All we need is an instrument to tune in to
them and then we can receive the broadcast wheather
it comes from the local TV station or from a near-
by C-B unit. As science advances with new tech-
nologies, they will discover new radio waves or
force fields and new uses of these fields. Many
other things that are unexplainable today will
come to light tomorrow.

What is the real purpose for all of these radio
waves and force fields around us? To me , these
currents are the GOD FORCE. They give substance
and life to all things. The trees, flowers,
grass, rocks and all things on earth and in the
solar system are made up of atoms. The individual
atoms are held together by a force to make a form,
shape and size that we can see and touch. The

current that flows through everything, that is
around everything, and touches everything is the
GOD FORCE. It is the cohesiveness that holds all
of these atoms together to give them their substance. Without this GOD FORCE all of these atoms
would just fall off into space. They would fly
away and would have no cohesiveness with each
other to form a rock or to make a tree. They
would be just atoms floating endlessly in space.
There would be no you and me.

This is not the only purpose of the GOD FORCE.
We cannot limit GOD, we cannot say that He is
nothing more than this. He is much more. It's
like the cable that the Telephone Company buries
in the street, it has the capacity to carry thousands of people's voices speaking at the same
time through it. The GOD FORCE is like this, it
has not only the capacity to hold atoms together,
but it also acts in many other aspects of our
life. Communication is a part of the GOD FORCE.
We are able to communicate with each other as we
are able to send our radio programs through these
waves or currents. We are also able to see and
to have light through these currents.

Science has found that light is vibration. They
don't know how it comes about or how this vibration works, but they do know that light is a
vibration.

In the Book of Genesis it was said, "In the beginning there was the WORD and the WORD was with GOD,
and the WORD was GOD." Words are vibrations, light
is vibration, and the GOD FORCE is light and vibration. We might change this to: "In the beginning there was VIBRATION and the VIBRATION was
with GOD, and the VIBRATION was GOD." Does this
make a little more sense? In the Bible we have
read many paragraphs like: "Let there be light",

"Man sees the Light of Christ , Christ is the
light of the World". Light is vibration and this
light is a part of the GOD FORCE. Like light,
the GOD FORCE always has been and always will be,
it is always there.

The GOD FORCE is like the river that flows from
the mountains down to the sea. It flows in its
natural course without any help from you or me,
and it will wind up in the sea no matter what.
We can dam it up but the more water that comes,
the sooner it will overflow and begin again its
trip to the sea. We can change its course,
divert it, or help it along, but it will flow and
reach its objective. It doesn't really make any
difference to the river whether we dam it up,
change its course, or try to stop it. It's going
to do just exactly what it has set its course to
do.

It's like the law of gravity. The law of gravity
operates regardless of how we feel about. We
drop a stone and it falls to the Earth. This is
the way the river is and the way the GOD FORCE is.
No matter what we think about it, no matter what
we try to do about it, it will continue doing what
it has done for countless aeons and will continue
doing this for countless more aeons, because it is
the GOD FORCE.

Only when we work within the Laws of the GOD FORCE,
when we move in the same direction as the rivers
current, or try to work with this current, are we
able to have the GOD FORCE work for us. If we try
to dam it up, to change its course, or to stop
it completely, we cannot succeed. We only succeed
when we work with the GOD FORCE LAWS, when we are
flowing with the current of the GOD FORCE and not
trying to set ourselves against it. Only then can
we succeed.

Now let's look at the GOD FORCE in a different
concept, the concept of size. In this physical
world of ours we see size in relation to ourselves. Things like tall skyscrapers are much
bigger than we are, and things like ants are much
smaller. This is our concept of size. In in-
vestigating dimension and size let's go further
than this, let's go to the smallest thing that we
know, "The Atom". Let's pretend for a moment
that we have the world's most scientific microscope. This microscope can see down further than
anything that has ever been invented. In fact,
there is no limit to this microscope. It can see
as far as we want to see down in size. Now let's
look at an Atom with our new microscope. We see
that this Atom has protons and neutrons circling
a nucleus. In the middle of this Atom is another
substance that looks like a ball of fire. (Science
is not quite sure what this ball is).

While we are looking at this Atom we suddenly discover that the ball of fire in the middle of the
Atom, looks just like a Sun, like our Sun. We
then discover that the things circling around this
Sun look like planets, like our planets.

Now let's pick out one of these planets, with our
super microscope, and 'zero in' on it to get a
real close view. In looking at this planet we find
that there are clouds on it, and there is water
and land. When we 'zero in' on the land masses,
we discover that on some land there are buildings,
houses, roads and even people.

With our fantastic microscope, we then look at a
beach on this planet. We 'zero in' on a grain of
sand on this beach, and we discover that this grain
of sand is made up of what looks like atoms. Then
looking at one of these atoms, we discover that it
has a middle with many things going around it . . .

This puts a new dimension to our understanding of size, doesn't it? And the GOD FORCE is in all of it, the currents that flow through everything also flow through our sub-universes. The GOD FORCE has no limits or boundries.

If we can go down in size with our new microscope, let's turn it around and now go up in size. We might discover that our planet and our Solar System may be nothing more than an Atom in someone else's planet and Solar System.

Looking up to the heavens where is the end? How far up can we go? And in all of this, both up and down, is the GOD FORCE. The energy field that flows through everything, holding everything together, giving us our life and our being.

So you see, the GOD FORCE is the currents and the energy fields around us. The FORCE that holds all of the atoms in the Universe (and other Universes) together and gives them their being. The FORCE that enables us to be human, to see light, to hear, and to live is the GOD FORCE.

ALL OF THIS INFORMATION IS JUST SO MUCH USELESS KNOWLEDGE IF WE DON'T APPLY IT AND USE IT IN OUR OWN LIVES. FOR TRULY THAT IS WHERE WE CAN DO THE MOST GOOD FOR MANKIND, TO WORK ON OURSELVES AND TO GET OUR LIVES STRAIGHT.

GOD FORCE

INVISIBLE CURRENTS

THE 'GOD FORCE' CURRENTS HOLD THE ATOMS OF OUR BODY TOGETHER!!

"THE GOD FORCE IS THE CURRENT AROUND US.
IT IS THE FORCE THAT HOLDS ALL OF THE ATOMS
IN THE UNIVERSE TOGETHER AND GIVES THEM
THEIR SHAPE, 'THEIR BEING'."

WHAT IS OUR HIGHER SELF ?

To understand what our Higher Self is, we must
have some understanding of the different levels of
consciousness. The average person is only conscious of things that are directly in front of
him. On rare occasions, he will have a flash of
knowing what someone else is thinking. Or he will
know what is going to happen before it happens.
This is another level of consciousness that he is
tapping into. It is a higher level of consciousness (a higher rate of vibration). You could compare these different levels to the different radio
frequencys. If you don't have the right radio,
you can't tune in the broadcast, you won't hear
anything.

Science tells us that plants and trees have their
own consciousness, as do the atoms in every living cell. Even the cells in our body have their
own individual consciousness.

Some people are aware of the vibrations in a room
as they walk in, or are aware of another person's
thinking before they say a thing. All of this is
a form of operating on a higher consciousness.
ESP is a form of a higher consciousness. Some
people can be aware of things going on in other
parts of the city or in other parts of the world
through their use of higher consciousness.

One afternoon, as I sat here writing this book, I
kept thinking about a river and a dam being built
to stop this river. I kept thinking that you can
not change the course of the river or dam it up,
so I added it to this book. The whole afternoon
my mind was on the dam not being able to hold the
river. The following day I discovered that a big
dam in Idaho had broken and there was great flood-
ing throughout that area. I must have tuned into a
higher plane of consciousness without really know-

ing it. My only explanation of this is that
these things were happening within the GOD FORCE
(within the currents around us), and that my mind
was tuned to a higher degree, enabling me to pick
up these vibrations. But it was not tuned up
high enough for me to recognize it and know what
was going on at the time.

Here on our physical plane there are many levels
of consciousness. What this means is that there
are many different levels of vibration. Rocks
are one of the most dense matter on the physical
plane, which means that their vibrations are the
most dense. The human body is less dense than
rock so it has a higher vibration than rock.
Water has a higher rate of vibration, as does gas
and even light. Light itself, has one of the
highest rate of vibration on the physical plane.

If we were to leave the physical plane and go into
other planes of consciousness, (in the spiritual
world) we would find that these worlds do actually
exist as does our own physical world, and they
exist right here beside us and around us. These
worlds exist on a higher rate of vibration. The
energy matter (or atoms), that exists on these
planes of consciousness, vibrate at a higher rate
of frequency. This higher frequency rate prevents
our eyes, on the physical plane (the slower frequency rate) from being able to see unless we are
tuned into them. It's on the same princible as a
dog whistle that can be heard by dogs, but not by
humans. This means that we must raise our rate of
vibration, and when we have done this, then we
will be able to see things in the spirtual world.
This, also, is the way that many people have seen
ghosts. At that time, they were tuned into a
higher rate of vibration.

If people can see ghosts and can hear spirit's
voices, as many readers can testify, then truly

there are other planes of existence that are on a
higher realm than our physical world. It is no
more than a higher rate of vibration. Each realm
of consciousness that is above the preceding
realm, operates on a little higher frequency vibration. Matter and energy on that plane of existence vibrate a little faster than the one below
it. On one of these higher planes of consciousness is where our true self rests.

What exactly is our Higher Self? In the Christian Church, as in many other religions, there is
the Trinity of Father, Son, and Holy Ghost. In
my explanation of GOD, I have come to feel that
the Holy Ghost of the Trinity is the GOD FORCE.
The Father would be the highest part of our Higher
Self, and the Son would be our lower self (our
personalities). There is a very fine line that
exists between our lower self and our Higher Self.
It's almost as if the Higher Self was divided into
many seperate parts, with the top most part being
a part of our Father in Heaven, which is pure consciousness. For the purposes of this Chapter, my
use of the words: Father in Heaven and Higher Self
shall have the same meaning. It is the highest
part of our Higher Self that is a part of our
Father in Heaven. It's as if there was a ladder
with the bottom step being our lower self and the
top step being our Father. It's still one ladder.

Like the GOD FORCE, our Highest Self (our Father
in Heaven) is always changing and always evolving.

In Darwin's Theory of Evolution, our physical
bodies have evolved from the primate in the sea,
to the stature of man that we are today. In many
religions it is taught that As above - So below,
which means that things are above in the same
order and under the same laws as they are below.
This would lead us to a logicial conclusion that
our Higher Self is also evolving just as our

physical bodies are evolving.

So what is this Higher Self that we have that operates and lives on a higher plane of consciousness? How does it communicate with us? How did it come to be?

These are some of the questions that I have tried to answer within myself, and this is the answer that I feel most comfortable with:

OUR HIGHER SELF (OUR FATHER IN HEAVEN) IS NOTHING BUT PURE CONSCIOUSNESS, WHICH MEANS IT IS EVERY-THING. IT IS COMPLETE IN ITSELF IN THAT IT KNOWS ALL, SEES ALL, AND IS ALL.

It operates within the Laws of the GOD FORCE. It is like the spark that is in the seed, and when the seed is planted, the spark knows when it is time to germinate, to spread its roots and start growing. It is the pure consciousness that meets in the mothers womb when the egg and sperm unite. It tells that sperm and egg, in its union, to form the beginning of a new life. This pure consciousness is what makes nature's abundance grow. It tells the trees when to shed their leaves and the birds when to fly south. All of the mysteries of birth, life, and death are complete and understood within the Father in Heaven (the Higher Self), this pure consciousness.

I believe that it was this Higher Self, the Father in Heaven that Christ refered to. It is the Father in Heaven that has always been and always shall be. It is this Higher Self, within each of us, that is ever evolving upward to a higher state of consciousness, higher than we can possibly concieve.

Our life here on the physical plane is nothing more than a point of expression for this pure

consciousness. We are the individual points of
expression for the Higher Self so that the good
that we do will proceed to the Father and the
Father will build upon this good. It's like the
cake that the master chef bakes, first he adds
the flour, then he adds the other ingredients.
As each ingredient is added to this cake in the
making, a little more flavor is added to it, and
a little more texture and a little different
taste. The more that is added to it, the more
the cake changes and takes form. Our Father in
Heaven is somewhat like this. The more we experience and the more good we do, is added to our
Father.

On this higher plane of consciousness, where our
Father in Heaven is pure consciousness, everything is one. Everything operates within the GOD
FORCE and is a part of the GOD FORCE. It's like
a drop of water that is separated from the ocean.
It has its own chemicals and its own special
ingredients, and they are completely different
from that of the ocean. When that drop of water
is put into the ocean, it merges with the ocean
and is no longer serparate from the ocean. On
the higher plane of consciousness where our
Father in Heaven operates, all is one, there is
no separates and no singleness.

In this brief explanation of these other planes
of consciousness, I would like to be sure that
my point is very clear. These other planes of
consciousness exist all around us right here
and now in this physical world that we live in.
They are not some place else, they are here, we
don't have to travel to another place to find
them. All we have to do is change our consciousness (tune in our receiver) to be aware of them.

These other realms of consciousness are exceed-
ingly important to us. These are the vast worlds

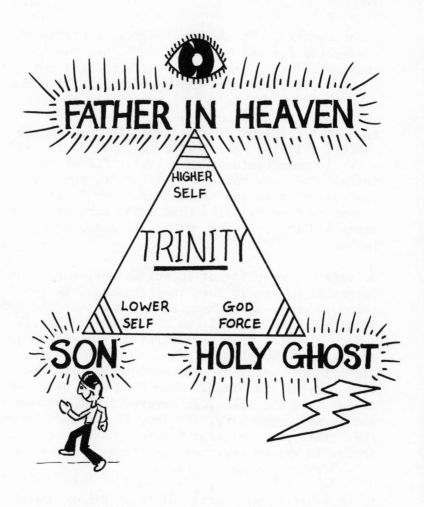

"THE TRINITY, SO OFTEN SPOKEN OF, IS OUR
HIGHER SELF, OUR PHYSICAL SELF, AND THE
GOD FORCE THAT HOLDS EVERYTHING TOGETHER."

of very picturesque and vivid life, and are the
places that we go between our physical lives.
The periods intervening between each life. It
is only our lack of development and our own lim-
itations, that are imposed by our human bodies
and minds, that prevent us from fully realizing
and seeing the highest glory of these heavens
that are around us here and now.

It is most important that everyone understand
that the use of the words higher and lower in reference to these planes, does not refer to any
position of one above the other. It is merely
just a degree of the frequency of vibration of
the matter that is on these different planes.
When a person goes from one plane to another, he
is merely changing his consciousness, changing
his vibrations so that he is able to operate and
have vision on this higher plateau of vibration.

This is how our Higher Self, (our Father in
Heaven) operates on a higher plane of consciousness. When we strengthen the link between our
Father and ourselves, we are able to bring our
relationship closer, we are able to hear the wee
small voice. And we are then on our way to becoming one with our Father in Heaven.

ALL OF THIS INFORMATION IS JUST SO MUCH USELESS
KNOWLEDGE IF WE DON'T APPLY IT AND USE IT IN OUR
OWN LIVES. FOR TRULY THAT IS WHERE WE CAN DO
THE MOST GOOD FOR MANKIND, TO WORK ON OURSELVES
AND GET OUR OWN LIVES STRAIGHT.

HOW WERE THE UNIVERSE, EARTH, AND MAN CREATED?

There is a story that is told about Ben Franklin,
it took place when he was living in France. The
story goes that there was a Frenchman who loved
to argue with Ben Franklin about the existence of
God. His argument was that there is no God, and
that man had just evolved from the apes. He was
sure that there was no Creator. One day Ben
Franklin hired a metal sculptor to make an exact
replica of our solar system. It was to be complete in every detail. After many months of work
and much money, the work of art was completed.
It was a magnificent thing of beauty. Mr.
Franklin put this grand piece in his front hall
and waited for the day that his Frenchman would
see it. That day came and the Frenchman couldn't
believe his eyes. He wanted to know where it
came from and who made it. Franklin's answer was
that it just appeared and that no one had made it.

The Frenchman replied, "How can this be, no thing
of beauty such as this can just appear out of no-
where?" Franklin answered, "Then how can you ac-
count for the original from which this was copied?
Did not someone make it?"

Man, since the beginning of time, has always won-
dered how he was created and how the world came
about. The Bible tells us that the beginning of
man was with Adam and Eve in the Garden of Eden.
And other religions teach similar beginnings. I
think that one of the most profound things that
has been theorized is that, "If there is a beginning, then the logical conclusion would be that
there must be an end. The Buddha taught that
anything created must have an end.

Our whole world is made up of many beginnings and
endings, and they are all preceeding one another
as a chain of events. Each link in this chain of

events is made up of its own beginning and ending.

Life, as we know it here on Earth, very well may
have an ending some day. However, that day is
surely far, far in the future. But this would
not be a complete ending, this would be just one
more link in the chain. And from that point, we
would go on to another beginning and ending of
another series of events and lives.

A great deal of information has been brought to
light in the studies of the history of our Earth.
Geologists have found many answers to questions
on the Earth's beginning, in rocks and fossils.
Science has discovered much about Earth and its
changes. There are several theories of the formation of our Solar System and of other solar
systems in our galaxy.

One of the most popular ideas on the formation
of our Solar System is the 'Dust Cloud Hypothesis'.
This theory suggests that rarefied dust clouds,
that float in outer space, are the birth places
of suns and planets. For periods over millions
of years long, they collect together and coagu-
late into denser groupings through the Law of
Attraction. They then set up new conditions
such as forming a more solid matter in their
mass, and as this process goes on, gravity comes
about through the movement of these formations.
This causes a concentration of the mass, and heat
and light develop from friction. A rotating
motion arises and throws rings of matter into
space as the central body shrinks further to become a future Sun.

All the while the lesser formations are spinning
around this new sun. These lesser formations
are moving at a great speed, hitting other par-
ticles in space, collecting them, and eventually

becoming larger. Through the rotation around the
sun, and with the sun's gravitational pull, they
develop into spheres, round balls of mass. And
as this mass slows down it finally develops its
own natural orbit according to its size and speed.
This is how, it is thought, that a solar system
comes into being. However, in the few short minutes it took to explain this, in actuality it
takes millions and millions of years to happen.

In coming to their scientific conclusions, they
completely leave out the idea or thoughts of a
Creating God. Scientific thoughts are that the
creation of a solar system is a natural evolution,
and up to a point I agree with this concept.
Everything is evolution, and everything is moving forward, however, I feel that it is moving
forward under the guidance and control of the
creative force of our Father In Heaven and of the
GOD FORCE.

As with our example of the links in the chain, we
also are fulfilling this concept as a link with
our solar system. It is merely a link in a chain
much bigger than we can imagine. All of the atoms
in the Universe, and all of the currents that flow
through everything are being held together by the
GOD FORCE, tying all of the links together.

Darwin's Theory of Evolution has brought science
to a new understanding of the creation and the
beginning of man. This Theory is in direct oppo-
sition to the beginning of man in the Garden of
Eden as is told in the Bible. One may ask, "How
does one justify these two concepts when they
are both opposed to each other?" I think to come
to an understanding with these two ideas, one
must look at them in a totally different manner.

The idea of evolution, as proposed by Darwin, is
correct from the standpoint of the physical

"OUR PHYSICAL BODIES DID EVOLVE FROM THE SEA,
AND OUR LOWER SELF WAS CREATED BY OUR FATHER
IN HEAVEN."

evolution of our bodies. Our bodies have evolved
upward from the sea, to the man that walks the
Earth today. But we are not our bodies, we are
something much higher and greater than our bodies.
The real "us" lives in our physical bodies, as
our bodies would live in a house, or drive in a
car.

When you point to a car, you don't say, "There is
John Smith." John Smith is in the car, he is not
the car. And so it is with our bodies, we are
not our bodies, we are in our bodies. Darwin's
Theory of Evolution is the evolution of our bodies
and not our real self.

It is stated in the Bible, that Man was created in
God's image. God does not have two arms or two
legs. He does not get athlete's foot, or have in-
grown toenails. God is not a man as we see men,
God is spirit. And he really isn't a He or She,
God is God.

We learned in a previous chapter of what God is,
so I will refrain from going over it again. However, using these ideas of God, we can see that
the creation and evolution of our physical bodies
under Darwin's Theory of Evolution, is correct.
The Bible's story of creation in the Garden of
Eden, is correct for the creation of our Souls,
or the joining of our souls to our physical bodies.
It would be this place in time when our Father in
Heaven breathed down His Life Force into the animal
bodies that were living on Earth. Giving these
bodies the ability to think and to be a part of
the Father. It is the story of the joining of
spirit and flesh, and the beginning of the union
on Earth.

You might compare this to the story of the evolution of the automobile. One of the first
autos was Henry Ford's Tin Lizzy. Through the

natural evolution of the automobile, we have come
to the sleek and fancy auto of today.

Here in the United States we do not go anywhere
without going in our auto. We drive our car to
work or to the shopping center. We turn corners,
change lanes, speed down highways, but yet we are
not our autos. We are human, and the auto is
nothing more than a piece of metal. So it is
with our physical bodies, they are nothing more
than flesh and bones.

We are not our physical bodies, we are much more
than that. We are spirit which is made in God's
image. We are one with the Father in Heaven. So
even though our physical body moves through the
World, maneuvering with speed and grace, we are
still separate from it.

The day that our spirit was joined to our physical
body was the day in the Garden of Eden. It was
that day that God breathed His Holy Breath into
those mounds of clay and gave them life, the day
that Spirit moved into the physical body.

This is how Man was created along with the scientific conclusions of how our Solar System and our
Earth were created. The GOD FORCE and our Father
in Heaven were there, taking a hand in the whole
matter.

ALL OF THIS INFORMATION IS JUST SO MUCH USELESS
KNOWLEDGE IF WE DON'T APPLY IT AND USE IT IN OUR
OWN LIVES. FOR TRULY THIS IS WHERE WE CAN DO THE
MOST GOOD FOR MANKIND, TO WORK ON OURSELVES AND
TO GET OUR LIVES STRAIGHT.

WHERE IS GOD ?

This is a question that has perplexed humanity
since the beginning of time. Everyone feels that
he should be able to see God and to know God, or
that God should show Himself to us. Whenever
there is a natural disaster, there is always someone to say, "It's the will of God". When good
fortune happens to someone, they usually say,
"God is smiling down on you". Maybe these people
are correct in what they say, but in a different
way than what they think.

The God that they refer to is on all planes of
consciousness. It is our Father in Heaven (which
is pure consciousness), is the God that they talk
about, and wonder why he doesn't show himself.

God does show himself to us, we just don't always
recognize Him. We watch a beautiful sunset, see
the miracle of birth, or observe other things of
wonderment all around us. We don't realize that
these things are really an expression of our
Father in Heaven, and that He is operating through
the Laws of the GOD FORCE. So you see, God does
show Himself to us everyday, all we have to do is
just turn around and there He is.

Another way that our Father shows Himself to us is
in our direct use of what Christ taught us, "AS
YOU SOW, SO SHALL YOU REAP." Through the use of
this Law, our Father is showing Himself to us by
giving us back exactly what we give.

When we give good to people, we get good back;
and when we give bad, that is also what we get
back. In other great religions around the world,
this is called the Law of Karma. I like to refer
to it as the Law of Cause and Effect.

Today there is much use of the word Karma and

"YOU REAP WHAT YOU SOW!!"

"THE LAWS OF CAUSE AND EFFECT ARE VERY CERTAIN SO BE CAREFUL OF THE THINGS THAT YOU SET IN MOTION."

many people are using this word without fully understanding it's total meaning. KARMA is a San-
skrit word which literally translated means
Action.   It is a fantastic law of opportunity.
"Whatsoever that we do to other people, we shall
have done unto us."

As Sir Issac Newton once said in his famous laws
of motion, "To every action, there is an equal
and opposite re-action." This, science tells us,
applies to all physical things of energy.

Timing is an aspect of the Law of Cause and
Effect which is quite often misunderstood. Things
returning to us sometimes return to us immediately,
or they could return to us later on in life, or
even in another life altogether. And as surely as
God is within us, it will come back. Just as a
seed that is sown in the ground does not spring
up and grow the next day; but waits until the
Spring, so it is with the Law of Cause and Effect
(Karma). It need not come right away, but it
does come in its own time and when the conditions
are just right.

St. Paul in his Epistle stated, "Be not deceived,
God is not mocked, for whatsoever a man soweth so
shall he also reap." Christ also said, in
Matthew; Chapter 7, "Judge no that ye be not
judged, for with what judgement ye judge, ye shall
be judged, and with what measure ye met, it shall
be measured to you again." Christ was teaching
the Law of Cause and Effect, the Law of Opportunity.

It is a Law of Opportunity because it shows us
that we are not in the grips of fate and we don't
have to follow the winds wherever they blow us.
We can make our own choice. This opportunity is
presented to us to give us a chance to correct
our mistakes. We are all human and do make mis-

takes, and these mistakes are corrected by throwing the same type of situations back at us to do
over again, and maybe the next time we will get
it right.

We reap only the things that we have sown. Another man may do us harm or a wrong which we think
that we don't deserve, and so he will have to pay
for this harm he has done. However, the law is
never wrong, we are never put in the position of
receiving something that we do not deserve. We
are never placed where we do not belong, or in
the path of anything coming our way that we do
not deserve. There is no such thing as accident,
chance, or luck; everything is as it should be.
Through our own free will and choice, we have the
opportunity to turn these situations to our gain
instead of a loss to us.

In the Bible, John; Chapter 9, we read: "And as
Jesus passed by he saw a man who was blind from
his birth and his Disciples asked him, 'Master,
who did sin, this man or his parents, that he
was born blind?' And Jesus answered, 'Neither
hath this man sinned nor his parents, but that
the works of God should be made manifest in him."
From this we see that not all difficult situations
are brought about through the workings of the Law
of Cause and Effect. The bling man, that Christ
refered to, was blind because his Father in Heaven
(his Higher Self) was giving him an opportunity to
climb a little higher on his evolutionary ladder,
by presenting him with a difficult task. If he
achieved it, (by living the best possible life),
then he would be able to scale the ladder a little
faster and come a little closer to his Father in
Heaven. This was the opportunity that he was given.

This example also shows that reincarnation was a
fact believed by many people back in Christ's
time. The Disciples believed in reincarnation for

they would not have asked Christ about the sins
of a man when they knew that he was born blind.
If there were no reincarnation a man would not
have been able to have sinned before he was born.
Christ, knowing and understanding reincarnation,
would not have answered in the way he did, he
would have flatly denied it.

The Law of Cause and Effect is not a series of
rewards and punishments, it is just our Fathers
plan whereby wrongs will be made right, and our
weaknesses will be turned into strengths, (but
only if we take the opportunities presented to us.

The Law of Cause and Effect is exact. There is
no fate, there is no chance, we get exactly what
we give. We reap as we sow. We have the opportunities to advance through the use of this law,
and whichever way we turn with these opportunities, it will be recorded in our future evolution.

It is through these opportunities that our FATHER
IN HEAVEN is showing Himself to us. He is always
near, all we have to do is see him and to listen
to him.   (Listen to the wee small voice within.)

ALL OF THIS INFORMATION IS JUST SO MUCH USELESS
KNOWLEDGE IF WE DON'T APPLY IT AND USE IT IN OUR
OWN LIVES. FOR TRULY THIS IS WHERE WE CAN DO THE
MOST GOOD FOR MANKIND, TO WORK ON OURSELVES AND
TO GET OUR LIVES STRAIGHT.

WHY IS MANKIND ALWAYS SEEKING GOD?

For thousands of years that he has roamed the
Earth, Mankind has been seeking God. There are
many reasons why we seek God, and some of the
reasons are better than others, but they all put
us a little closer to God.

Before we can explain the reasons, we must first
define what it is we are seeking. Is it the GOD
FORCE or is it the Father in Heaven that we are
seeking? As you have read, the GOD FORCE is the
current that keeps everything together and is
the Universal Law. Our Father is PURE CONSCIOUS-
NESS, and the spark that is in the hidden mysteries of Nature. Therefore, when we say that we
are seeking God, we really mean that we are seeking the FATHER.

There are many reasons that philosophers and
great thinkers of the world have given for mankind to seek the FATHER. Some of the reasons
that they have given are:

1. Man seeks GOD out of Fear, fear of the
   unknown, and fear of Hell.
2. Man seeks GOD to build his own Ego.
3. Man seeks GOD out of habit of seeking GOD.
4. Man seeks GOD for his own security.
5. Man seeks GOD to better himself.
6. Man seeks GOD to help others.
7. Man seeks GOD for the love of GOD.
8. Man seeks GOD to become One with GOD.
9. Man seeks GOD to return to the source
   from which he came.

The first reason why people seek the FATHER is
out of fear of the unknown and fear of a burning
Hell. Over hundreds of years, there have been
many religious preachers that have taught the
people to fear God and to fear the fires of Hell.

This has always been a good way to keep the masses in line. By putting fear in the people, they
would be afraid not to do what is right.

There really is no need to fear God, for we are
really pure light, and an expression of our FATHER.
We are a physical point of contact for our Father
in Heaven. By being a part of our FATHER, we are
GODS without even knowing it. However, even our
FATHER must follow his own laws and the laws of
the GOD FORCE. So when we wrong our fellow man,
we must pay for it. Normally, that payment is in
kind. But when our wrongs have been so great that
we could not possibly repay them, then sometimes
we have to wash these wrongs away and start all
over again with a fresh slate.

The second reason people are seeking God is to
build their own ego. These are the people who
pray in Church on Sunday and wrong their fellow
man on Monday. They put people down to show how
righteous they are. These people don't know who
and what they are and they don't realize who or
what their FATHER is. Time will tell and their
evolution will be. Everyone, at some period in
time, (or in another life) will work their way into a higher state of consciousness and to a higher knowledge. At some life or another, a person
must blossom as a flower blossoms when it is the
right time. Therefore, seeking God to build one's
own ego is nothing more than moving on the path
and taking the first step up the ladder towards
our FATHER.

The third reason that people seek God is out of
habit. This habit of seeking God has come by
way of the ego. They sought God to build their
ego, and this seeking became a habit with them.
A habit of going to Church on Sunday, or going to
Bible meetings, or praying. And with this habit,
they are moving up to the second step on the

ladder to God.

The fourth reason for seeking God is for security.
When a person does not want to burn in hell, and
wants to be secure where he is, then he will go
out of his way to do what is right. Psycholog-
ists tell us that we must feel secure in what we
are doing, and we must feel a sense of security
in all things around us. And seeking God gives
us this sense of security. We now move up another
step, on the ladder, closer to our FATHER.

The fifth reason we seek God is to help ourselves.
This is where the teachings of many religions have
been used for man's betterment. We are taught
that if we repent and ask forgiveness of our sins
and live the good and pure life, then when we die
we will go to heaven and live on streets paved
with gold. We will have Angels serving us and
will be the favorites in God's eyes. By doing
this, we are trying to advance ourselves in God's
eyes. We are trying to move forward. In other
words, we are helping ourselves and moving up
another step on the ladder.

The sixth reason we seek God is to help others.
We have been told that doing things merely for
ourselves is selfish. As we advance on the path,
we step aside from our selfish attitudes and seek
to help others. Down deep, we really know that
when we help others, we are also helping ourselves.
The further along that we move on the path, the
more we discover that helping others is just another expression of love. Loving others is just
another expression of our loving God. And this
moves us even closer to the top of the ladder.

The seventh reason we seek God is for the love of
God. For the seventh we can combine the next two
reasons into one higher reason for seeking God.
We find that loving God is not enough for us, we

must also become one with God. When we seek to
become one with God, we soon discover that our
final reason for seeking God is to return to the
source, return to our FATHER IN HEAVEN. And this
puts us at the top of the ladder with God.

These are the basic reasons why we seek God.
The mistake that many people make is seeking God
elsewhere when he is really inside of us all of
the time.

I have said that the last reason for seeking
God was to <u>return</u> to our source and to become
one with God. I will try to explain this idea
with the following example.

Let's for a moment think of a light bulb, and
imagine that this bulb has its own individual
consciousness. Imagine that it is a separate
entity of its own. Our light bulb also has a
thinking process of its own. As it sits there
in the lamp, it thinks that it is really the
light. It feels that all light comes from it.
Our bulb doesn't know that it's not really the
light, but is merely a point of expression for
the real current that flows from the plug in the
wall. And the house current is not the real
current that lights the light, it's just an expression of the transformer that's on the pole
in the street.

The transformer is not the real current that
provides the light for this bulb, it's just an
expression of the power that comes from the generator at the Light Company. This generator is
not the source of the electricity that lights
the light, it's an expression of the people who
work for the Light Company to produce the electricity. And they are an expression of their
FATHER IN HEAVEN. So where does the light come
from that lights this light bulb, and where does

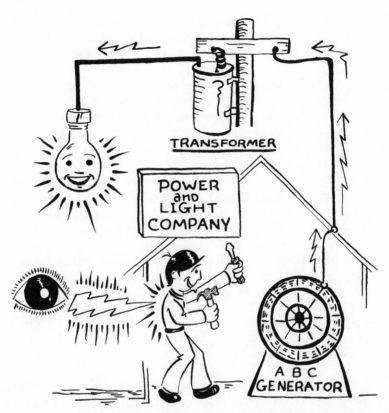

"WHERE DID THE POWER COME FROM??"

"THE POWER THAT LIGHTS OUR LIGHT IS NOT
REALLY COMING FROM US. IT COMES FROM OUR
FATHER IN HEAVEN. WE ARE REALLY AN EX-
PRESSION OF OUR FATHER AND DON'T KNOW IT."

it have its beginning? Our light bulb that thinks
that it is the light, is merely a point of expression for the current that flows through it.

Our FATHER created us to gain wisdom, knowledge,
and experience so that we and He may grow. We are
not really us, we are really His point of expression, and His point of consciousness. We are
really one with the FATHER and we don't know it.
I'm sure that this must be a very different idea
and concept to grasp. We are so use to thinking
of our own individual selves, seperate from one
another, that now to think we are all really one
with the FATHER, makes it hard to understand.

The hardships and challenges of our daily lives
are nothing more than golden opportunities for us
to grow. We grow with these hardships because
they are friction, and "<u>Without friction, there is
no growth</u>." The seed must push its way through
the earth to become the lovely flower. It can not
grow without friction.

Let's imagine, for a moment, that our scientists
have developed and built a brand new computer.
This computer is so fantastic and powerful that it
has the ability to do things far greater than any
other computer has ever done. All of the knowledge of all of our books, science and technology
has been programed into this computer so that it
has on its memory banks, all of the knowledge of
the world.

This computer fills a complete room and is almost
perfect in every way, except that it has a person
in another room feeding it information.

Our computer thinks that all of the thoughts and
all of the information that comes to it are coming
from itself. And to some extent, it is correct
because it operates its own mechanisms within.

"EACH OF US HAS A CONNECTION TO EVERYONE ELSE. WHEN WE HURT SOMEONE, WE ARE ALSO HURTING OURSELF."

This truly is a marvelous machine, but without the
operator that operates it in the other room, and
without the electric current that runs through it
and gives it its power, our computer would not be
anything at all.

This also is our situation, without our FATHER pro-
gramming us and without the GOD FORCE giving us
the life current, we would be nothing at all.

Deep within every one of us we know our relationship with the FATHER, we know that we would be
nothing without Him. So we are constantly striv-
ing to make that connection with Him, a little
stronger. A little stronger for our own security,
for our own ego, or for whatever the reason may
be. And this is why mankind is constantly searching for Him. In all of the new thought magazines
and books, and everywhere you go, you will find
someone searching for GOD, that's why you are
reading this book now. And some day, we will all
find Him.

How do you express a story or describe something
that there are no words for? How do you describe
a feeling, a knowing or something within you that
is so fantastically tremendous that there are no
words to describe it? How do you put something
like this down on paper. How can you describe it
so that people will understand, so that they will
know and see what you see? How can you paint a
picture of a sunset that expresses the feeling
that you have within you when you witness this
glorious and beautiful sunset? How can you paint
a spine tingling event? How do you put this
knowledge to words? Poets, writers and philosophers of all ages have tried.

This deep feeling within us, this feeling that is
impossible to describe, is really our feelings

about God, (our seeking God). When we see these
beautiful sunsets, we are really seeing God in
His role as Nature. This deep feeling that we
are haveing is just our way of seeking GOD.

FATHER, I AM THEE AND THEE AM I,

I THINK THAT I AM I, BUT I AM NOT I,

I AM THEE AND ME.

FOR THEE AND ME AM I !!!!

All of this information is just so much useless
knowledge if we don't apply it and use it in our
own lives. For truly this is where we can do
the most good for mankind, to work on ourselves
and to get our own lives straight.

VI

WHAT LAWS CONTROL OUR LIVES ?

There are many laws that control and/or operate in
the physical world as well as in the spiritual
world, and I will only talk about just a few of
these here in this chapter. Some of these laws
that will be discussed are the laws of Cause and
Effect, the laws of Attraction, the laws of Cycles
and the physical laws of science, used in our
everyday life.

Let's begin with the law of Cause and Effect.
This is the law that you read a little about in a
past chapter. Here are a few more ideas for your
inspection.

As you will remember, the main thing about this
law is that "As you sow, so shall you reap", you
can't plant corn and expect to have potatoes or
wheat. Every time that you do something, you must
realize and expect, that the same type of thing is
going to come back to you. Whether it be good or
bad, it's the law of Cause and Effect, it will
come back to you, action and re-action.

Criminals dislike societies laws because they prevent them from expressing their selfish desires.
The same laws make good citizens feel secure and
safe in the knowledge that these laws are there to
protect them. And so it is with the law of Cause
and Effect. These laws are there to help and to
protect us and give us the very best if we are
good citizens. But if we are bad citizens, then
the laws of Cause and Effect will be our pay mas-
ters. They work for us or against us in direct
proporation to what we give, therefore, good
citizens need not fear the law.

The law of Cause and Effect works in many aspects
of our life; in our health, our work, finances,
and our family relationships.

Our health is controlled by the law in the way our
minds work. As we think, so goes our health. The
word "disease" is an excellent example of this.
The word disease comes from two other words; 'dis'
meaning out of, and 'ease' meaning relaxed.
Usually when we have a disease it is because we
aren't relaxed in our mind and our body. When we
think healthy thoughts, we are healthy. As we
think, so shall it be, it's the law of Cause and
Effect.

In our work and in our finances, we find the same
thing. Whatever we put into them is what we get
out of them. If we're lazy, holding back and don't
really put forth our very best effort at our job,
or if we try to hide from our boss and just get by,
then that's exactly what our life will be: Just
getting by. We won't be able to have the riches
and fulfillment of what we could have, unless, we
give the best in our thoughts and our actions.
Those who really put forth the greatest effort,
who unselfishly give of themselves to their job
and to their family are the ones that get back,
from life, exactly what they have given. When
they give thoughts and actions of love, they get
back love.

The law of Cause and Effect operates on all planes
of consciousness, this means that it also applies
to what we think. When we think of doing something
good for someone, but our thoughts come from selfish motives like expecting some reward for this
good, then it will backfire on us. In this case,
our thoughts are the controlling factor in the law
of Cause and Effect. Good actions must be given
without any selfish thoughts of achieving something.

In our thoughts, we cannot expect to give something
that we think has no value, for something that has
value. This is why confidence men are able to Con
people out of their money. These victims are seek-

ing to get something for nothing. <u>There is no
such thing as something for nothing</u>. You have
earned, at some time or another (or even another
life), everything you get. And if you haven't
earned it, then you will have to pay for it some-
time in the future (or even another life). Nothing can come to you without having to pay the
bill, either before you get it, or after you get
it. The bill must be paid. But sometimes that
bill is paid by others. An example of this would
be if you gave something of value to friend 'A',
then later, something of value came back to you
from friend 'B'. The law brought back to you,
what you gave, but from a different source.

Another law that controls our life is the law of
Attraction. This is the law that science has
demonstrated with the action of the magnet. The
magnet is a piece of iron that has the power and
ability to attract other iron. It will not attract
copper, gold, silver, or aluminum. It only attracts iron, <u>it attracts what it is</u>. The law of
attraction works daily in our lives. Just by looking around us, we can see the type of people that
are attracted to us. This is the type of person
we are. Whatever they are is what we are, we are
attracting them to us and they are attracting us
to them.

Criminals associate with other criminals, sick
people attract other sick people, professional
people seek other professional people. Whatever
you are is what is attracted to you, and is what
attracts you. If you don't like your life, or the
people that you associate with, then change your
attitudes, personality, or the way you think.
Change yourself and these people will drop away
from you. You will become a different person,
attracting different people and different surroundings to you.

"IT'S THE LAW OF ATTRACTION, <u>LIKE ATTRACTS LIKE</u>. WHATEVER YOU ARE IS WHAT YOU ARE ATTRACTED TO, AND WHAT IS ATTRACTED TO YOU. IF YOU DON'T LIKE WHAT IS ATTRACTED TO YOU, CHANGE YOUR LIFE !!!!!

There is a story of a farmer back in the pioneer
days. This farmer was sitting on the front porch
of his farm when a covered wagon rolled by and
stopped at his front gate. The man driving the
wagon asked the farmer, "What kind of people live
around here? We have left our past behind us and
are moving West to find a new home." The farmer
looked at them and asked, "What kind of people
were in the town that you left?" "Why, they were
nasty and suspicious people, and very hard to get
along with," said the man in the wagon. So the
farmer replied, "Well, that's exactly the kind of
people that live around here." And the man in
the covered wagon drove on, looking for another
place to settle.

A few days later, another wagon came by and stopped at the farmers gate. The man in the wagon
also asked what kind of people live around here.
The farmer looked at this man and asked, "What
kind of people were in the town that you left?"
And the man answered, "Why, they were good people,
honest, God fearing and kind." So the farmer
replied to this man, "Well, that's the same kind
of people that are around here."

Whatever you have left behind is what you're
going to find ahead, unless you change the way
you think. It's the law of Attraction, like attracts like. If you are a loving, kind and good
person, that's what you will be attracted to and
what is attracted to you. This is also a form of
the law of Cause and Effect, what you give, is
what you get back.

Another law that we live under is the law of
Cycles. The law that says that there is a time
and a place for all things. A season for everything, a season for planting and a season for har-
vesting.

Our physical bodies are controlled by the physical, emotional, and mental cycles. The physical cycle is a 23 day cycle, the emotional cycle is 28 days, and the mental cycle is 32 days. These are the cycles science has discovered that operate within our bodies. They are called the Cycles of Biorhythms.

The Science of Biorhythms is a theory of statistical probability which is claimed by it's advocates to be capable of indicating a person's physical, emotional and intellectual states within the time cycle. It is based on the theory that man is living on three rhythms with his day of birth as the starting point.

Astrology is another law of Cycles. As our astrological planets move from one house to the next, they bring forth different effects upon our body, mind and emotions. These are the cycles of birth, life, and death.

Everywhere you turn, you will see things working in cycles, and these cycles can work for - with - or against us whichever we choose. We just don't put on our bathing suits to go out and shovel snow.

There are many physical laws that science has proven throughout the ages. Some of these laws are: The law of Gravity; The laws of Energy and Matter; The laws of Motion; Thermodynamics laws; and the laws of electricity and magnetism. Some of these physical laws relate to higher spiritual laws. The law of Gravity is a physical law working as the law of Attraction and the law of Cause and Effect. You cause a ball to go up in the air by throwing it, and the effect is that it comes back down, it is attracted to the ground.

Water seeking it's own level is an application of

the law of Attraction.

These are just a few of the many laws that control our lives. What I have done here is try to
give you an idea of the basic laws that effect
our lives daily, and how they apply to us.

Who made these laws? Is God the one that controls them?

As we have learned in past chapters, the GOD
FORCE is the Law, and doesn't have to think about
being something other than LAW, or being anything
less, it just is. Our Father in Heaven, knowing
these laws, and understanding the GOD FORCE,
operates within these Laws to gain experience for
us and for Himself.

The LAWS come from the GOD FORCE, and are used by
our FATHER and our Higher Self, to put new experiences on our table of life.

Are you starting to get the feeling that there is
really something more than just our own individual personalities? Something more than just YOU
and I?

ALL OF THIS INFORMATION IS JUST SO MUCH USELESS
KNOWLEDGE IF WE DON'T APPLY IT AND USE IT IN OUR
OWN LIVES. FOR TRULY THIS IS WHERE WE CAN DO THE
MOST GOOD FOR MANKIND, TO WORK ON OURSELVES AND
TO GET OUR LIVES STRAIGHT.

WHAT IS OUR MIND ?

What and where is our mind and what powers does it have? Many people believe that their mind is the thinking part within their head, and that the mind is the brain. There are those who believe that the mind is their own true self (their higher soul) Doctors have not been able to find the mind located anywhere in our physical body. They know that it does exist, but not where it's located.

Most all of my teachers have taught that the mind is separate from the body. It is not a part of the brain, yet the mind uses the brain as we would use a computer. We program information into a computer, and punch buttons to get information out of it. The brain is also a computer, a very marvelous and magnificent computer. And this computer is operated and controled by our mind. All of the bodily functions and reflexes that our computer operates are programmed and set into motion by our minds. There have been many cases of Yogis who were able to control bodily functions through the use of their minds. Some have even been able to stop their heart beat.

Our mind is not our body or our brain, it is not a physical object, it is much higher than this. Our mind should be considered as the vehicle to which our FATHER IN HEAVEN manifests Himself as intellect. Within this intellect we have developed the powers of the mind which include those of memory and imagination. And this, in the later stages of man's evolution, will serve as a separate and distinct vehicle of consciousness in which man can live and function quite apart from his physical body.

Many people do not exercise their mental abilities as much as they should. Their minds become receptacles rather than creators. Constantly

accepting other people's thoughts instead of forming their own from within. A realization of this
fact should induce a person to change his attitudes in his daily life and to watch the working
of his mind.

One of the best things that I have read on the
development of the mind was in E. Norman Pearson's
book, "Space, Time and Self". In it, he states
that with each lifetime there are many changes that
take place in the development of our minds. Our
minds begin in the infancy state and change into
childhood, from childhood we change to adolescence, and from adolescence we change to maturity,
and then to old age. Each age presents a particular set of problems for a person to face.

From birth to the age of seven, the physical body
is developing. In this period, the foundations of
physical health and strength for the entire life
are to be laid down. It is very important that a
child be given every opportunity for a healthful
exercise in the open air and sunshine without un-
necessary restraint. While the need for simple,
early mental training and education may be felt,
it should not be allowed to interfere with partic-
ipation of outdoor activities.

From the ages of seven to fourteen years, it is
the period that marks the growth of the emotional
nature of the child. During this time the child
can be appealed to primarily through its feelings.
Care should be exercised that such appeals do not
violate reason. Education should be concentrated
on the emotional rather than the mental growth of
the child. The almost total lack of such guidance
in our present day educational systems and schools
has resulted in many wasted years, resulting in a
lack of emotional control in later life. There
should be wise guidance of the child's emotional
nature, into desireable channels to avoid many

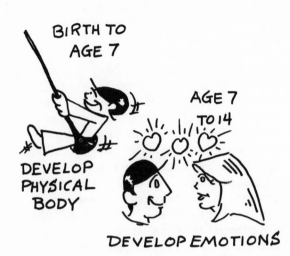

BIRTH TO
AGE 7

DEVELOP
PHYSICAL
BODY

AGE 7
TO 14

DEVELOP EMOTIONS

STAGES OF A CHILD'S GROWTH AND DEVELOPMENT

AGE 14
TO 21

DEVELOP
MIND

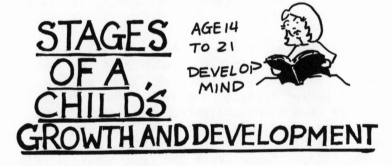

"IN EACH LIFETIME THERE ARE MANY CHANGES THAT
TAKE PLACE IN THE DEVELOPMENT OF OUR MINDS.
THIS IS WHY IT IS SO IMPORTANT THAT WE DO A
GOOD JOB IN THE DEVELOPMENT OF OUR CHILDREN."

mistakes in the future. This is essentially when
religious teaching, in its most idealistic concept
of love and devotion, will be of great value to
the child.

From the ages of 14 to 21, the intellect takes the
lead in the expanding picture of the life of the
child. The key note of this period is that of
rapid growth of the mental faculty. Study and
concentration in school are high on the list of
important things in the development of the child.
But even more important, are the powers of analytical thinking and reasoning. With the background
of religious teaching, and the development of
analytical thinking and reasoning, will lead the
child to further accomplishments in maturing on
its own. It might be mentioned in passing, that
some authorities consider that maturity is reached
at the age of 18.

These few years, it can be observed, make a great
deal of difference in the unfolding of the mental
powers, the reason for which should be evident.
In this period religion should be lead into the
paths of reason and enlightenment, yet, without
losing any of its quality of true devotion. When
a man reasons he is adding something of his own
to the information contributed from outside. His
mind works on the materials supplied to it, and it
links the perceptions together, blending the various sensations into one.

Our minds could be likened to the point on a pencil. It writes on a piece of paper but it is
guided by the hand of God. And with this connection with God, it becomes an expression of God.
An expression of our Father in Heaven. Our FATHER
is not visible, He is not seen by our physical eye.
Our mind, also, is not seen by our physical eye,
but yet it is there. It is there as our point,
and His point of contact with our physical body.

There is a strong working connection between our brain and our mind. When our hand touches a hot flame, the nerve centers in our hand send that heat sensation through our nervous system to our brain. Our brain immediately reacts with motor response. Triggering another sensation to our hand and to our arm, which withdraws our hand from that flame immediately. There is no thinking needed, this is an automatic response.

But is it really, is it really an automatic response programmed by our brain to trigger this type of reaction? The breathing that the body does is also called an automatic reaction. Taking air into the lungs and then expelling it out is thought to be purely automatic and not under our conscious control. However, there have been many Yogis from India and even from the West, who have demonstrated the ability to stop their breathing. To stop the normal body functions, and to even stop the automatic functioning of their heart, and then restart it again under conscious control.

If this were possible, and it has been demonstrated in many scientific laboratories, then it means that these individuals are using their mind to control their body functions, functions that have in the past, been determined to be automatically controlled by the brain. And this too would indicate that the mind is controlling the body through the use of the brain. If all of this is true, and I believe that it is, then our automatic reflex of taking our hand away from the hot flame is not an automatic reflex. It is an action that has come about through the use of the mind. From our subconscious mind to our brain, a signal comes saying that this flame is hot, get our hand away from it, and immediately the brain is triggered into action and pulls the hand away from the flame.

Yogi Philosophy teaches that basically man's mind
can be separated into three sections, or planes of
mental effort. These planes are called:
    1. The Lower Subconscious Mind or Instinc-
        tive Mind, (which is the lowest).
    2. The Conscious Reasoning Mind or Intellect.
    3. The Superconscious Mind or the Spiritual
        Mind, (which is the highest and a part of
        our FATHER IN HEAVEN).

THE INSTINCTIVE MIND is the lowest of the three
planes of mental effort. It is important that we
understand that there is not a definite separation
between these three functions. We may think of it
either as one mind functioning along three lines,
or as three minds shading into each other.

The Instinctive Mind is the first plane reached in
the scale of evolution, and is the plane we share
with lower animals. The work of our bodies is
performed by this part of the mind. The constant
work of repair, replacement, digestion, etc., all
below the plane of consciousness. It is the seat
of the appetites, passions, desires, instincts,
sensations, feelings, and emotions of the lower
order, manifested in man as well as in the lower
animals.

Instinctive mind manifests varying degrees of consciousness, varing from almost absolute subcon-
sciousness to the simple consciousness of the highest of the lower animals and the lower forms of
man. Many men are but little more than animals,
and their minds function almost entirely upon the
instinctive plane.

It is astonishing how many of our daily tasks are
performed under the direction of our instinctive
mind, subject merely to a casual supervision of
the Intellect. When we learn to do things "by
heart," we have really mastered them on the

Intellectual plane, and then passed them on to
the instinctive mind. (This is also the "habit"
mind.

The Instinctive mind is most useful to man in
this stage of his development. He could not exist
as a physical being without it, in fact, he may
make a most valuable servant of it if he under-
stands it. But woe to him who allows it to remain in control.

There is no violent change or marked transition
from the consciousness of the Instinctive Mind
to the Intellectual Mind. As the INTELLECT unfolds, it endows instinctive life with reason.
Before the development of intellect, a creature
would have passions but no reason; emotions but
not intellect; desires but no rationalized will.

INTELLECT is the dawning of self-consciousness.
Without self-consciousness, a creature may know;
but only with the aid of self-consciousness is it
possible for him to know that he knows.

Simple consciousness is an awareness of outside
things, a perception and recognition of things
other than the inner self. The conscious attention is turned outward. The animal (or low order
of man), cannot think of his hopes and fears, his
aspirations, his plans, his thoughts, and then
compare them with the thoughts of others of his
kind. He can't turn his gaze inward and speculate
upon abstract things. He simply takes things for
granted and asks no questions. He does not at-
tempt to find solutions for questions within himself, (he is not even aware that such questions
exist).

With the advent of self-consciousness, man begins
to form a conception of the "I". He begins to
compare himself with others and to reason about it.

The awakening of intellect does not necessarily
make a man a better being, in the sense of being
good. While it is true that an unfolding of the
intellect faculty will give an upward tendency to
man, it is equally true that some men are so close-
ly wrapped in the folds of the animal instincts,
and the material side of things, that the awakened
intellect only tends to give them increased powers to gratify their low desires. The higher the
degree of intellect unfolded in a man, the greater
the depths of low passions, appetites, and desires
possible to him.

The brute nature may exert a pull downward, but
the SPIRITUAL MIND will give a helping hand up.
It will sustain you if you but trust it. The
intellect is between the two, and may be influ-
enced by either or both, take your choice.

All that has come to man, in his evolution, which
tends toward nobility, true religious feeling,
kindness, humanity, justice, unselfish love, mercy,
sympathy, etc., has come to him through his slowly
unfolding SPIRITUAL MIND. His love of God and his
love of man has come to him in this way. All that
we consider good, noble, and great in the human
mind emanates from the SPIRITUAL MIND and is gradually unfolded into the ordinary consciousness.

The Spiritual Mind is also a part of our FATHER,
and is His means of communicating with the Intellectual consciousness. He passes down to the
Intellect certain truths and the Intellect reasons
about them. But they do not originate with Intellect. Intellect is cold, spiritual consciousness
is warm and alive with high feeling. Man does not
become kind or loving by cold reasoning. He becomes kind and loving because there arises within
him certain impulses and desires coming from some
unknown place, which render it impossible for him
to be otherwise without suffering discomfort and

pain.

While the actual existence of the Spiritual Mind
has been made manifest to but a limited number of
the human race, there are many who are becoming
conscious of a higher "Something Within", which
leads them up to higher and nobler thoughts,
desires, aspirations, and deeds.

There is an old story of each person having two
advisors, one at each ear, his angel self whis-
pering to him to follow the higher teachings and
his devil self tempting him to pursue the lower
path. This is nothing more than the Intellect
being pulled by the INSTINCTIVE MIND on the lower
side and the SPIRITUAL MIND on the higher side.
The struggle between the higher and lower natures
of man have been studied by many observers of the
human mind and character.

The Spiritual Mind is also the source of the in-
spiration which poets, painters, writers, and
preachers have received in all times. This is
the source from which the seers and prophets obtain
their visions. Much that man has attributed to
outside intelligences has really come from himself.

When man learns of the existence of his Spiritual
Mind and begins to recognize its promptings and
leadings, he strengthens his bond of communication
with it, and consequently receives light of a
greater brilliancy. When we learn to trust the
FATHER, he responds by sending us more frequent
flashes of illumination and enlightenment. As one
unfolds in Spiritual Consciousness, he relies more
upon this Inner Voice, and is able more readily to
distinguish it from impulses from the lower planes
of the mind.

Knowledge is power; learn to know the remnants of
the brute nature within you and become a tamer of

wild beasts.

It has been proven that <u>Thought concentrating it-</u>
<u>self attentively on any idea, builds that idea in-</u>
<u>to the character of the Thinker</u>. A man can create
in himself any desired quality by sustained and
attentive thinking. In other words, you can be
anything you want, good or bad, by sustained concentration on that object.

When the connection, between our Spiritual Mind
and our Intellect, is made stronger, then more
information passes down from our FATHER to the
Intellect. This information comes quite often in
dreams or meditation. It is often used as a helpful hint or a way of providing help to the thinker.

What are the powers of the mind? What hidden po-
tentials do we have within us that gives us fantastic powers? We've all read about people who
have fantastic powers of ESP, those who can see
things that are happening in other places without
being there. People who know of things that are
going to happen, or tell other people about their
past and their future. These are all different
powers of the mind. There is also the power of
healing. One of our greatest Healers was Jesus,
the Christ, who also had the power of bringing the
dead back to life.

There are yogis who can stop their heart beat, who
can walk on red hot coals without burning their
feet. Some can even stick needles into their bodies without feeling pain or showing blood. Walking
on water, materializing things from the air and
many other things are also the fantastic powers of
the mind.

And Christ said, "ALL THESE THINGS THAT I DO, YOU
ALSO CAN DO AND MUCH MORE THAN I." Why would he
have said this if he did not mean it? It is also

written in the Bible, "Ye can move mountains if Ye
will." Are not all of these things powers of the
mind? Abilities that are latent within all of us,
abilities that we can do if we really use our
minds the way others have done.

There have been many cases where people under hypnosis have been able to do strange feats that they
could not have done while awake. A popular trick
of stage hypnotists is to have a subject face the
large audience for a second. The subject is then
told to turn his back to the audience, and then he
is asked to tell how many people are in the audience. The subject, without pausing, will tell
exactly the number of people present. Is this not
another power of the mind?

The powers of the mind are unlimited. The mind is
not physical and therefore has no physical bound-
aries. It can come and go at any speed, and in
any direction that it chooses. It's only limitat-
ion is us, is our ability to use the mind to its
full capacity as many people have done throughout
history and even in the present day.

One of the main obstacles to our being able to use
all of the powers of our mind is that our minds
are untrained. They lack the ability to concentrate on one subject for any length of time. Our
minds jump around from one thing to another, faster
than lightening. Just like a monkey in a cage,
jumping around from one spot to the next. Untrained and undisciplined, jumping from one pleasure to
the next.

Notice how a successful man is able to keep his
concentration on one job at a time till it comes
to a satisfactory conclusion. Just like a magnify-
ing glass condenses the sunlight into a single beam
to enable it to start a fire. That is the power
of the trained and concentrated mind.

VIII

WHAT HAPPENS WHEN WE DIE?

WHERE DO WE GO WHEN WE DIE - AND HOW LONG DO WE STAY THERE? The Christian religion teaches that only the good will go to heaven and those who are bad and evil, will go to Hell. They also teach that there are many degrees of Hell. Many other religions teach different things.

In looking at all of these different religions and comparing them with each other, we find that there are many different opinions of where we go when we die. The only thing that they do have in common is that a person goes someplace else when he dies. Some believe that this is the only human life that we live, and others believe that we live many human lives. Still other religions believe that we may live many human lives and many animal lives.

If reincarnation is a fact, then we will come back to another human life. But, in the meantime, where do we go when we are not in our physical body? The only real conclusion that we can come to is that there are many places that we go between our human lives.

There are many philosophies and many religions that hold to the concept that there are different levels of consciousness or planes of existence within our realm of living. It is somewhat difficult to understand these planes of existence or divisions. The essence or matter on these appropriate planes, has a certain degree of density, also this essence, or matter, is interpenetrating the matter of the plane next below and above it.

It should be clearly understood that the words higher and lower, (above and below), with reference to these divisions or planes, does not refer in any way to their position. They all occupy the

"WHERE DO WE
GO WHEN WE
DIE?"

"IN THE DEATH PROCESS OF MAN, SOME RELIGIONS
SAY THAT A GOOD PERSON WILL GO TO A CITY THAT
HAS STREETS PAVED WITH GOLD".

same space, but only to the degree of rarity of
the matter of which they are respectively composed.
In other words, the matter is vibrating at a higher
rate of frequency on a higher plane. Therefore,
the higher the plane, the higher the vibration.
It follows that if you speak of passing from one of
these planes to another, it does not mean that
there is any movement in space, but simply a change
in consciousness and vibration. Everyone has matter within him that belongs to each one of these
planes of consciousness, and each of us has a vehicle that is corresponding to these planes of consciousness. In other words, we have many bodies
within our body.

In order to pass from one of these planes to another, you must change the focus of consciousness
from one of these bodies to another, and use the
body of that plane of consciousness.

I'm sure that we have all read of the ghosts that
haunt the castles in Europe. These ghosts have a
very fine body that allows our material body to
pass right through. An explanation of this would
be that they are actual people who have dropped
their physical bodies, and have passed on to a
higher realm, to a higher rate of vibration in another body. And when other people see ghosts,
they are really seeing the body of that higher vibration. Just as we have many things that vibrate
on a higher and lower rate of frequency here in
the physical world, so it is on other planes of
consciousness. They are operating at a higher
rate of frequency and the matter within these
planes is less dense than physical matter.

Christ said, "In my Father's House there are many
mansions, and there I go to prepare a place for
you". What he meant was that there are many planes
of consciousness, different levels of vibration
and awareness for us to go when we drop our physical

bodies.

Some religions describe man as going to cities
with streets of gold. Other descriptions are
that we spend our lives, on the other side, with
our loved ones who have passed on before us. It
is also taught that if we spend our life harming
others, then most certainly we would find ourselves in a form of Hell, having to repay for the
harm that we did to others.

If reincarnation is a fact, as I believe it to be,
then we have lived not only lives of our present
race, but also lives of other races. We have been
black, white, red, yellow, and who knows, maybe
even green.

Reincarnation is probably the one single thought
that can make the most complete revelation in
man's outlook on life than any other thought we
can have. Scientific research has investigated
into man's early history and into the history of
the human race. As we look at our television
sets, we watch the episodes of these ancestors.
How startling this would be if we discovered that
it was not really stories of our ancestors, but
actually our own lives being shown on TV. What
if we were really the ones that roamed the open
spaces, or lived in caves, tents, or covered
wagons.

Race after race, life after life, we lived, died
and were born again. We hunted, fought and raised
our families in the manner of those early times.
Little by little we advanced our knowledge, and
our living conditions slowly improved. Century
after century has slipped away and gradually we
have climbed upward on the ladder of evolution.

Reincarnation is a teaching that once was accepted
throughout the world, but was lost to the Western

world when it was condemned by the Roman Catholic
Church back in the middle 6th Century. Although
commonly rejected throughout Europe and America,
reincarnation is accepted by the majority of mankind throughout the World, today and in all of
the past centuries.

Throughout our life we constantly see reincarnation taking place wherever we look. Rain is reincarnated as it drops from the clouds to the Earth,
runs to the ocean, evaporates back into the clouds,
and then rains down upon us again. Daylight is
reincarnated every 24 hours. The mighty oak tree,
in the Fall, drops all of it's leaves, dies and is
reincarnated again in the Spring. Before the tree
itself dies, it drops an acorn to the ground which
comes forth as a new oak tree.

Our seasons are reincarnated every year through
the cycle of Spring, Summer, Fall and Winter. As
it is with things around us, so it is with us.
Man can never die, his soul (or his mind, which
ever you care to call it.) is that eternal spark
within him that lives on and on, evolving upward.

Does it make sense for our FATHER to have put us
on this Earth for seventy some years just to learn
to be good people within those few short years?
I think not, I think that our soul is evolving
just as our body is evolving. Our bodies have
taken millions of years evolving to what we are
today. And so it is with our souls, we must have
taken millions of years evolving to what we are
today, we must have many experiences, which means
many lives. It is a logical conclusion to come
to, and that is that we have lived many lives in
the past, and that reincarnation (as belived by
the majority of the world) is a fact.

Thousands of years ago, Egyptians were buried in
their tombs with their possessions so that when

they awakened on the other side they could have
their possessions to use in the other world. This
is what they believed. The American Indian believed that when they died, they would go to their
happy hunting grounds, and would live a life
similar to that which they were living here in
the physical world. Some Eastern religions teach
that when a person dies, he will awaken with his
ancestors.

Throughout the world, there are many different
ideas of where we go when we die. Which one of
them is correct? How could they all possible be
correct?

Most all of my teachings have been that "IT IS
OUR THOUGHTS AND OUR PAST DEEDS THAT CONTROL
WHERE WE WILL GO WHEN WE DIE." If we were born
in the East, and believe as the Eastern Religions
and cultures teach, then this is where our
thoughts will be. We are the ones who control
our destiny. We will go to the place where we
think we will go. If we wish to be on streets
paved with gold, that is exactly where we will be.

There are two parts to this; our thoughts and our
PAST DEEDS. If we have some bad deeds to repay,
for wrongs that we have done to others, then our
thoughts will take us where we can repay these
bad deeds. And in some cases, that will be to
some form of Hell. Here again, the controlling
factor is our thoughts, thoughts from our higher
self. In most all cultures and religious teachings, we are taught that we must pay for our sins.

It is the law of Cause and Effect that we must
pay our debts, (we can't get something for nothing). So the thoughts, of our higher self, will
take us to the place where we can repay these
debts. Whatever part of the world that we are
living at the time of our death, or whatever

our culture or religious belief we have, is exactly where our thoughts will be. We will go to the
place that we think we will go. This is why all
teachings are correct. It is our thoughts and our
past deeds that control where we go when we die.

The time that we spend between lives will vary for
different individuals. It will also vary under
different circumstances. The two things that play
the strongest part in determining how long our
stay will be, are; OUR DESIRES AND OUR PAST DEEDS,
(The laws of Attraction and the laws of Cause and
Effect). By desiring to remain in a happy state on
another plane of consciousness, we will do so until
our desires turn to the physical life. Once our
thoughts are directed here, and the law of Cause
and Effect is ready for us to learn again, then we
will be placed in a position for learning new experiences and reaping what we have sown. Both
things are what determine how long our stay will
be before our next rebirth. For different individuals it is a different length of time. It is not
one set time for all, as it is not one set place
where everyone will go.

It is important to understand that it is not someone or something else that puts us where we will
go, nor is it a place set aside for us to go. It
is our own higher self, our spiritual mind, that
directs us to the place that <u>IT</u> has created.
Everything is Thought, and through Thought everything is created.

<u>YOU REALLY DO CONTROL YOUR OWN DESTINY</u>.

ALL OF THIS INFORMATION IS JUST SO MUCH USELESS
KNOWLEDGE IF WE DON'T APPLY IT AND USE IT IN OUR
OWN LIVES. FOR TRULY THIS IS WHERE WE CAN DO THE
MOST GOOD FOR MANKIND, TO WORK ON OURSELVES, AND
TO KNOW THE WORKINGS OF OUR OWN MIND.

REINCARNATION, TRANSMIGRATION AND EVOLUTION

Before we can have any serious discussion about
reincarnation, transmigration and evolution, we
must first define these words in the context that
we will be using them.

For our purpose here, we shall define the word
reincarnation to mean: A person, after dying and
being reborn, is reborn in a human form on this
physical plane. This means that a person would
come back as a person and not as an animal or any
other form of life.

Our definition of transmigration will mean that a
person could come back as a human, an animal, an
insect or any other type of living form (excluding
plants). It would mean that a person can have
one life as a human, one life as an animal, back
to human, to insect, back to animal, or back to
human.

Our definition of evolution shall be the standard
Webster's Dictionary definition. By this we mean
that a person is evolving not only with his physical body, but also with his spiritual growth.

As we have seen in previous chapters, reincarnation is something that is believed by the majority
of the world. However, many also believe in transmigration. Reincarnation was originally in the
Christian Bible, but was taken out in the early
history of Christianity.

The main question that we have before us is,
whether reincarnation is a fact or transmigration
is a fact? Many find it hard to believe in the
idea of transmigration. They find it hard to
believe that they have ever been an animal or
that they will ever be one in some future life.

REINCARNATION OR TRANSMIGRATION?

WHICH IS CORRECT?

"BELIEVING IN REINCARNATION IS MOST DIFFICULT FOR SOME PEOPLE, AND TRANSMIGRATION IS EVEN HARDER TO BELIEVE IN".

There is a philosophy that teaches, that anything
lower than human life has what is called a "GROUP
SOUL". By this they mean, that all dogs have a
common Group Soul, as would all fish, birds or
insects.

An analogy to this Group Soul theory would be to
have a bucket of water represent the Group Soul.
Then put many glasses around this bucket of water
to represent the many different individual animals of that one species. We would then take
water from the bucket and put some into each individual glass. Into each glass, we would put a
different colored dye. One glass of water would
be colored red, another blue, and so on. After
all glasses have been filled and colored, ·we
would then empty each glass back into the bucket,
one by one. As we would empty each colored glass
of water back into the bucket, the water in the
bucket would change color.

The Group Soul theory is that each individual
animal (a glass of colored water) has gained some
experiences and knowledge (the colored dye)
through its life, which is brought back to the
Group Soul (the bucket of water) when it dies.
All animals, in that Group Soul, would benefit
from the experiences and knowledge gained from an
individual animal. This is what we would call
instinct, and this instinct was learned from other
animals, of that same species, within the same
Group Soul.

Have you ever seen a school of fish swimming in
the water? The school consists of hundreds of
fish swimming together in unison, with all fish
going in the same direction. They all turn at the
same time, and even reverse without bumping or
touching each other. It is as if they are all
part of the same life and had the same mind within
them.

Have you ever seen a flock of birds in the sky,
where there seems to be thousands of birds flying
together? The same thing happens with the birds
as with the fish, they seem to move and fly together without bumping into each other. It would
be impossible for a group of people, even in half
the numbers, to move in unison as fish or birds do
without running over each other. This certainly
does give weight to the Group Soul theory.

The Group Soul theory goes on to suggest that the
life force, in each of us, has evolved up through
the Group Souls of the Mineral Kingdom, Plant Kingdom, Animal Kingdom and then individualized into
a human life.

What effect does the law of Cause and Effect play
on reincarnation? Under the theory of Cause and
Effect, if a person did many wrongs to his fellow
man, during his lifetime, then he would be put
into a situation where these wrongs would be paid
back to him in another life.

Believing in the idea of reincarnation is very
difficult for some people. Of all the religious
doctrines in the world, I would think that reincarnation is the one that is the most hotly contested.

Back in the 6th Century A.D., the Catholic Counsel
of Constantinople declared that all references,
in the Bible and elsewhere, to reincarnation
should be taken out, and that the idea of reincarnation was not a valid thing for the Church to believe in. As we have seen in previous chapters,
they were not completely successful, and there are
still many references, in the Bible, left to give
evidence of the original belief in reincarnation.

In Matthew, Chapter 5:48, Christ gave this command
to His followers, "Be ye therefore perfect even as

"MANY GLASSES FROM THE GROUP SOUL!!"

"THE GROUP SOUL THEORY IS THAT EACH INDIVIDUAL ANIMAL SOUL HAS GAINED SOME EXPERIENCES AND KNOWLEDGE IN ITS LIFE. AND AT DEATH, THIS KNOWLEDGE IS ADDED BACK INTO THE GROUP SOUL FOR THE BENEFIT OF THE OTHERS. THIS IS ALSO CALLED INSTINCT".

your Father in Heaven is perfect." This command
from Christ would be impossible for anyone to complete if there were only one life here on Earth.
We must have many times at bat to gain this perfection, and Christ knew that we would need many
lives to acquire this perfection.

There can be found many other places in the Bible
that support the idea of reincarnation. The theory
of God's justice is a good example for believing
in reincarnation. All of mankind wants to believe
that GOD is a good, loving and just GOD. That HE
is not passing out favors to one person and punishment to another. But what about the child that
is born deformed, blind or handicapped? What was
the purpose for this handicap? GOD IS a good,
loving and just GOD, He does not put these things
on a person just to see if they can work their
way out of them, or to see if they can learn to
live with their handicaps. Life is too short for
that.

The logical conclusion is that these people were
born with their handicaps because they are working
within the Law of Cause and Effect from their
deeds of a previous life. Their handicaps are the
opportunities for advancement that they have
earned for this lifetime. There is no such thing
as punishment from GOD. He only gives us what we
have earned. The opportunities that we have earned.

Another thought for reincarnation is the birth of
many gifted children. Some children have been
born with a musical aptitude, and can sit down and
play the piano without ever having studied music,
and they play brilliantly. And many others have
been born with other great talents. Is it not
logical to assume that they have learned these
talents and abilities in a former life? And that
this knowledge is just a return of their former
abilities. Old knowledge is quickly relearned.

We often see people who seem to catch on quickly, and quickly adapt to difficult things, with seemingly effortless ability. Would this not be knowledge that has been learned before, learned in a past life, which is now coming forth in this life?

Another item that is in defense of reincarnation would be the countless articles in newspapers, magazines and books referring to specific people and dates, who have remembered their past lives. The case of Bridey Murphy is a documented case. It is a story of a woman, under hypnosis, who recalls her previous life in Ireland.

There is a case recorded in India where a young Hindu girl of eight years of age, recalled her former life in a town just a hundred miles away from where she lived. She described the town and her home. She described the people around this town, her husband, her children and everyone in detail. The amazing thing about this case was that she had reincarnated just a little over two years after her death. And the people whom she had lived with were still alive.

Upon learning of this incident, investigators were sent out to discover the truth of this girl's story. They found the former husband, friends, and relatives of this girl and brought them back to her for examination. Upon seeing her former husband, the young girl burst into tears and bowed her head in respect. When she was questioned as to who the people were, she had no hesitation and quickly identified all. Further investigation of this girl's story proved that all of the facts she gave concerning her life were accurate in all details.

Another story that was printed in a magazine article, was about a three year old Indian boy who recalled his past life in a distant town in India.

He gave quite extensive detailed descriptions of
his life as a boy growing up and then as a man in
this town. Later, with investigators, he went to
this town to see if what he had said could be prov-
en to be correct. All of the things that he said,
including the schoolhouse and his former home, were
there and as complete as he had described them.
A photograph of the boy's former class was found
and was shown to him for identification. The boy
quickly identified all of the members in the class,
including the picture of himself, which subsequen-
tly proved to be true.

Another story of reincarnation appeared in a Ger-
man Weekly magazine in 1967. It was about a woman
who realized that she had lived another life. The
article tells how she and her husband were taking
a motor trip across Germany, and into areas where
she had never been. They came to a town that she
seemed to recognize, and she suddenly cried out
that this was the town where she had lived before
as a young peasant girl before World War II. She
remembered all details about the town, her home,
friends, and family.

This was something quite new to her and her husband
so they set out to prove or disprove these facts.
The town was as she remembered with a few changes.
They then entered a completely unchanged village
tavern, and the owner was the same man she knew in
her last life. After talking to him for some time,
he verified all of the details that she had told
her husband. He even told them how this young
girl had died in an accident.

There are many more cases like these, documented,
investigated, and found to be completely authentic
in every detail. Even the Dahali Lama's, of Tibet,
own personal story relates how he has reincarnated
many times into his present life as The Dahali Lama.

One must come to a logical conclusion that reincarnation is a fact. However, the main problem
people have in believing in reincarnation, is not
reincarnation itself, but their confusion with
transmigration. Do we really go back from man to
animal, and animal to man? With all of the cases
that have come to light of people remembering
their former lives, there has never been one case
where a person remembers his life as an animal,
(to the best of this author's knowledge).

The Group Soul Theory seems to be a very logical
theory, yet the idea of wiping away our bad debts
also seems very logical from the standpoint of our
transmigrating into animal or insect lives. So
what is the answer, where does the truth lie?
The Buddist's idea of transmigration is their way.
The Theosophical idea of Group Soul and no transmigration is their way. And who can say for certain that either one of them or both of them are
right or wrong?

After much deliberation on this, I have come to
my own truth. For me, both of these ideas are
correct, (to some extent). There is something
within me that really objects to having to go
back to an animal existence. I feel that I have
climbed the ladder of evolution and that going
backwards to an animal existence is like climbing
down the ladder. The truth that I have come to,
(now) lies right in the middle of Reincarnation,
Transmigration, Evolution, and the Group Soul
theory.

Man is on an upward path in his spiritual growth,
but sometimes that upward trend is not quite as
discernable as in other times. Sometimes it even
looks like it is going down. It's an upward
spiral, like a bed-spring sitting on its end.
That spiral has a definate trend, moving in a
circle upwards. However, if you look at this

spiral with a microscope, you would see that this
definite trend upward is not clearly discernable.
You would see pits and small jagged mountains. It
would look like a Stock Market Chart of ups and
downs. I think that our spiritual evolution is
very much like this spring. It has a general trend
upward, however, each individual lifetime may have
it's own up or down trend like our stock market
chart. But still the general trend is always on
an upward direction.

The idea of going backwards into animal existence,
WITHOUT ANY REASON, does not fit into my theory.
Part of this theory involves the Law of Attraction
and the Law of Cause and Effect. I feel that when
a person, through his thoughts and deeds, has led
a grossly animal existence in this lifetime, then
under the Law of Attraction, all of those gross
thoughts and deeds would be attracting gross animal atoms to him. When this person dies, the magnetic action of the Law of Attraction and the Law
of Cause and Effect would be working for him. And
this grossly animal type person will come back with
an animal body that would fit his thoughts and
deeds. This also works for the person whose
thoughts and deeds have been high and good. The
vibrations that are impressed upon him will cause
him to be attracted to only good atoms, and will
bring about a fine life in a fine body for his
next life. When the period of rebirth comes to
these different individuals, through the Laws of
Attraction and Cause and Effect, they will be reincarnated into the body that they have been
attracting and have earned.

The Group Soul of animals, or other different
species, will continue to grow and will continue
to evolve till it has reached the maturity where
it will be given the SPARK OF LIFE from our Father
in Heaven. And that Spark will change this Group
Soul into an evolutionary being that will

reincarnate on the path upward, through many lives
till it becomes one with the Father in Heaven.
And this, also, is the path that we have taken to
reach our present point of Spiritual Evolution.

No matter whether it is reincarnation, transmigration or the group soul theory, the main reason
that we are here is to get our act together. To
learn how to deal with our problems, and to move
on to the next set of problems. <u>There NEVER will
be a time when we are finished dealing with prob-
lems</u>. Once we have learned to handle the problems
that we are now dealing with, we will then be
given a new set to work with. And if we don't
learn to deal with these problems before we die,
then we will come back again to these same type
of problems until we can handle them. Our real
growth and learning truly comes from the way that
we deal with our problems. The final score doesn't
count, its the way we play the game. And this is
why I keep repeating that:

ALL OF THIS INFORMATION IS JUST SO MUCH USELESS
KNOWLEDGE IF WE DON'T APPLY IT AND USE IT IN OUR
OWN LIVES. FOR TRULY THIS IS WHERE WE CAN DO THE
MOST GOOD FOR MANKIND, TO WORK ON OURSELVES AND
TO GET OUR OWN LIVES STRAIGHT.

WHAT CONTROLS OUR NEXT BIRTH?

What controls our next birth, and do we have any choice in the matter?

The Smith family, down the street, have just had a new baby boy. He was born to them last week. Mother and baby are very healthy and doing fine, and Mr. Smith is a very proud new father.

But, let's pause here for a moment and turn the clock back in time. Back before the birth of their child. Back an undeterminable amount of time, (with each person the rebirth time is different.) We'll go back to when this new baby boy, of the Smith family, was a man living in another lifetime.

What was the reason this man reincarnated into the Smith family? Why did he go to them instead of to the Jones family, down the street? Or to any other family in any other part of the World?

I think that what it is that tells us where to reincarnate is nothing more than the Laws of Attraction and the Law of Cause and Effect. The Law of Cause and Effect, also, has a strong pulling power for us. This means that if we have wronged a member of our family, or someone else, and if this wrong remains unsettled at the time of our physical death, then this creates a magnetic attraction that we will have for this person because we have not paid our debt to them. This attraction will pull us back to them so that we can have another chance to settle our debt.

In the Old Testament it was taught, "An eye for an eye", and then Christ came and taught that you should love your enemy. What these two teachings are trying to teach us is the workings of the Law of Cause and Effect. I think that what the Old

Testament really meant when it said, an eye for an
eye, was that if you give bad, you must get a return of bad. It may not be from that person that
you did the wrong to, but somewhere around the cor-
ner you must receive a return of that bad. I believe that Christ was trying to tell us to love
our enemies so that we would not create any bad
that would have to come back to us. So that we
would not reap the same that our enemies are reaping. Christ also taught that you "Reap what you
sow". If our enemies are giving us wrongs, then
they will definately reap what they have sown.
He was telling us to love our enemies so that we
will reap the love that we have sown. This, also,
is true about our thoughts, so be careful of what
you think, it too will come back to you.

Everything going out must come back, be it actions
or thoughts. If we send wrongs in repayment of a
wrong, then that is what will come back to us.
But, if we do not send a wrong, and instead we
send love in repayment of a wrong, then we will
get love back (but it may not be from our enemies).
And those who have wronged us will get their wrong
back, but from someone else.

We are connected to our Father in Heaven, and all
that we do, He knows. All that we experience, He
also experiences. There is no escape, no getting
away from what we do or think. All of our wrongs
must be righted. The Law of Attraction and the
Law of Cause and Effect, are two things that dictate where we will be reborn. To what family we
will come and what our next life will be like.

Children who are born with great abilities and
talents that far exceed the average, are born into
families who are interested in the same things,
(in most cases). For instance, a child who has a
very good music ability, is normally born into a

family that has a high interest in music. And so
it goes with all other fields. There are many
great movie stars who have children, who have also
taken acting as their career, and have proven to
be great stars in their own right. This is not
an accident, it is due to the law of Attraction.

A soul is drawn to a particular family because
this is the experience that they want to have for
this lifetime. They have come here, through this
attraction, to develop their talents and to further their understanding and learning. If they
were to come into another family, that was not in
the same field of endevor, then they would not
have that opportunity to express themselves and
to grow. They would not have the coaching or tu-
toring that parents must show to these young
children.

Like attracts like, what these souls are is what
they are attracted to. That, also, is the reason
for so many father and son businesses. It is so
very important for a parent to give his child as
much of himself as he can, to give him training
and as much knowledge as he can. This is one of
the reasons why that child came to those parents,
to learn and to further his knowledge.

Like attracting like is not the only reason why a
soul would come to a certain set of parents. Another reason would be under the law of Cause and
Effect. If there was a situation that was not
settled, or a wrong that was not righted, then
this would also be the attraction for an entity
to another.

Two brothers who have fought with each other all
of their lives, would again be attracted to each
other for this reason. Their fighting and dislike for each other, in this life, undoubtedly
was because of some animosity they shared in a

past life. Now they are coming face to face,
again, to try to work this situation out, and if
they don't work it out in this life, then in another life they will be brought together again.
It may not be as brothers, it may be as sisters,
or as parent and child. But in any case, they
will be brought together again so that they will
have the opportunity to work out these differen-
ces. They will have to keep coming back to each
other until it is settled.

Our Higher Self (Our Father in Heaven) keeps our
ledger sheet, He knows to who we owe debts, and
who owes debts to us. He knows what we are stri-
ving for, and what new things we are to learn.
He is keeping all of our records and is leading
us in the direction that will advance us the
fastest. And he puts us on the path that would
be the most beneficial for our development.

As we gain in our spiritual knowledge and growth,
we too can help our Father in making our own
choices, regarding our lives. It could be our
decision as to which parents to come to when we
have developed far enough on the path and our
spiritual growth has been far above average.
Otherwise, it would be left in the hands of Our
Higher Self. Really and truly, could there be
any better Hands to leave this decision in?

ALL OF THIS INFORMATION IS JUST SO MUCH USELESS
KNOWLEDGE IF WE DON'T APPLY IT AND USE IT IN OUR
OWN LIVES. FOR TRULY THIS IS WHERE WE CAN DO THE
MOST GOOD FOR MANKIND, TO WORK ON OURSELVES AND
TO GET OUR OWN LIVES STRAIGHT.

FREE WILL AND CHOICE, OR PREDESTINATION?

Is there such a thing as predestination or do we have free will and choice with our lives?

Predestination or free will and choice have been hotly contested throughout the ages. There have even been songs written that say, "What will be, will be". Is our destiny already written, and are we just following through life doing what has already been predestined? There are religious teachers who teach that God's will is devine, and that God decides all factors for us, however, they still sprinkle in some ideas that we have free will and choice to choose between good and evil.

Those who believe in predestination believe that our lives have already been set down in God's Book. They feel certain that everything we've planned to do has already been written and that there is no way that we can avoid our destiny. If we were meant to be teachers, we would be, or if we were meant to be engineers, this also is what we would be. Our whole life would be following God's master plan.

Those who believe in predestination are also convinced that, in our lives, if we were to come to a fork in the road, it would already be predetermined which direction we would follow. That we would really have no choice in the matter. It would already be known which decision we would make, and which path we would follow. Nothing would be left to chance.

Another idea of predestination would suggest that each life is different. Some lives are good and some are bad. It is for us to learn to overcome the challenges that God has placed before us. We

must overcome these hardships and learn to live
with them, within our destiny. It would be said
that God is not being discriminatory towards one
person or another, and that everyone has good
lives and bad lives to live. How they use them
and what they do with them is to their credit or
to their detriment. Each one of us would have
the same opportunities.

If predestination were a fact, one could almost
say that God was handing out favors to some, and
denying others. That God had already decided
how good or how bad we were going to be. We would
have no 'say' in the matter, whatsoever. This
type of situation would tend to leave one feeling
that he might as well give up even before he
started, that his destination is already set, and
whatever happens is going to happen. So why try,
why try to do better, or live a better life, or
work harder, or do anything. Life is already set
the way it's going to be and no matter what we do,
that's the way it would be.

The other side of the coin is 'Free Will and
Choice'. Those who believe in free will and
choice say that God created us so that we could
live our own life and find our own way through our
free will and choice. They say that God has the
power and ability to dictate man's lives, but that
he doesn't interfer. Free will and choice has
been left to us to learn from our mistakes and to
strive to better ourselves in every way. It would
be like taking a trip from Chicago to Detroit. We
have a road map on our lap and we see the best
route to take to Detroit. We follow the highway
that is shown on the map, and we end up in Detroit
just as the map indicates. However, we have free
will and choice. We can take a side road, off the
main highway, and see the country on the way to
Detroit. We can enjoy the scenic view that we

IF YOU CAN CUT YOUR STRINGS OF PREDESTINATION —
—YOU WILL HAVE
"FREE WILL AND CHOICE"

"THE PREDESTINATION THAT WE ARE LIVING TODAY, IS NOTHING MORE THAN A REFLECTION OF YESTERDAY. WE ARE REAPING WHAT WE HAVE SOWN. WE NOW HAVE FREE WILL AND CHOICE TO SOW GOOD SEEDS WHICH WILL BE OUR PREDESTINATION FOR TOMORROW."

would not have seen if we had stayed on the main
highway. It would take us a little bit longer to
get there, but we would have a lot more experiences and learn a lot more from the trip by using
our free will and choice. That's the way that
people, who believe in free will and choice, feel
about their lives.

Like so many things around us, there is always
two sides to a question. Two definite opinions.
Also, like so many other things, they are both
right, there is truth on both sides of the coin.
The answer to the question; which is true, predestination or free will and choice?, lies in
both opinions. They are both correct. How can
this be, you ask? How can both extremes of the
pole be correct when they lie in opposite direct-
ions?

Predestination is true, because what we see as
predestination is nothing more than the workings
of the Laws of Cause and Effect. What we've set
in motion at one time, MUST have it's effects in
another time. The good that we do must be re-
warded, just as the wrongs that we do must come
back to us. WHAT GOES OUT MUST COME BACK. Our
lives are predestined to follow the Laws of Cause
and Effect, for certainly we must reap what WE
have sown.

The predestination that we are living today, (our
lives as we see them now) is nothing more than the
reaping of what we have sown in the past. We
caused what we are doing today, by our actions of
yesterday. If we are receiving good today, it is
only because we gave good in the past, (and that
past could have been in another life). This is
the way that it is with all things around us.
The child protege who sits down at the piano and
plays like we have never heard before, is a pro-
duct of has former life.

The practice, work, and the achievement that he carried with him from that past lifetime, shows in this lifetime. <u>The life that we are living today is our predestination from yesterday</u>. Our life has been written down, but it was us who did the writing.

How does free will and choice fit into this? How are we able to move from these predestined paths, onto paths of our own choice?

We can do this by doing no wrong to others, by setting no bad entries on our records that we will have to repay. We must watch what comes from us, watch everything that we talk and even think about. We must try to make our actions and our lives a little bit better, and one of the ways to do this is to follow an old rule that was taught long ago. "DO UNTO OTHERS AS YOU WOULD HAVE OTHERS DO UNTO YOU." How can you sow a bad seed by following this rule? We would still be under the laws of predestination, but it would be the destiny of our own choosing.

As long as we can live by the Golden Rule, which most all of the religions teach, then we can move around in the world without creating any bad effects for our next life. We will only create good effects.

It is our actual choosing (our free will and choice) to plant no bad seeds, to give only good, that makes our predestination the way that we would want it. <u>What we are now doing, saying, and thinking is our future destiny</u>.

Once we have mastered ourselves, we can then master our surroundings and our future. That will be when we find that predestination has no further effects on our lives, and our lives will be ruled by free will and choice.

Our predestination was not set by God, it was
set by us. It was set by our own Free Will and
Choice. So watch what you do, say, and think,
because you are setting your predestination for
tomorrow.

ALL OF THIS INFORMATION IS JUST SO MUCH USELESS
KNOWLEDGE IF WE DON'T APPLY IT AND USE IT IN OUR
OWN LIVES. FOR TRULY THIS IS WHERE WE CAN DO
THE MOST GOOD FOR MANKIND, TO WORK ON OURSELVES
AND TO GET OUR OWN LIVES IN ORDER.

WHAT IS LOVE ?

Love is a word that is very difficult to define,
it has many meanings. Love is so strong that people have killed for love, and wars were started
for love. Even the Bible tells us that the world
and universe began from love. Christ said, "A new
commandment I give unto you, that ye love one another as I have loved you." He also said, "Thou
shalt love thy Lord thy God with all thy heart,
with all thy soul and with all thy mind. This is
the first and great commandment, and the second is
liken unto it. Thou shalt love thy neighbor as
thyself."

There are many types of love. For the purposes of
this book, I have categorized these different types
of love into four categories. They are:

1. THE LOVE OF PLEASURE.
2. THE LOVE OF SELF.
3. PARENTAL LOVE.
4. SPIRITUAL LOVE.

THE LOVE OF PLEASURE can be for many things. Some
of the things in this category, would be our love
for good food, nice clothes, a nice car, a good
home, loving companions, and anything that we could
have a physical attachment for.

THE LOVE OF SELF concerns our ego. It is our own
self esteem and the way that we feel about ourself.
It's the feeling that we get when someone tries to
get in line ahead of us, or tries to move around us
to take advantage of us.

PARENTAL LOVE is our love for our children, the
feeling that we have for them, and the wishes we
have for their well being. It is the protective
instinct that mothers have for their children.

<u>SPIRITUAL LOVE</u> is our love of GOD, our love for
a Higher Being, and a higher force. It is our
love of nature, and the worship we express in our
Churches and our Religions.

Love needs something or someone as an object for
its expression. It needs to be directed towards
something, whether that something is an idea, a
person, place, or thing, it must have a direction
to travel.

To aid in my definition of love, I have separated
these four types of love into two divisions:
Higher Love, and Lower Love. In the Lower Love, I
have included the love of pleasures, and the love
of self. In the Higher Love, I have included the
parental love, and the spiritual love.

<u>LOWER LOVE</u> is an attachment to people or things.
It is our expectations as to how they should act
to please us. When they please us, we honor them
with our love. If they do not meet our expectations, we do not honor them with our love.

<u>HIGHER LOVE</u> has no attachments, it is a true love,
a pure love. Higher Love is the giving of our
love without expecting anything in return. Lower
Love always expects something in return. Higher
Love is the sending out good feelings, the sending
out of good wishes of well being to someone, without any attachments or hopes of rewards. It is
very important that this love be given without any
expectations or hopes of reward coming back to the
giver. It cannot be, I'll love you if you love me.
It must be, I'll love you even if you don't love
me. This is what makes it a Higher Love instead
of a lower love.

Love is an emotion, and emotions are strong feelings within us. Emotions can be broken down into

LOVE OF:
1. CHILDREN & FAMILY
2. NATURE & BEAUTY
3. GOD & RELIGIONS

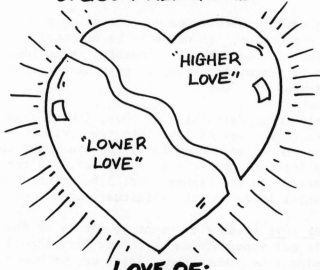

LOVE OF:
1. PHYSICAL PLEASURES
2. OTHER PLEASURES
3. SELF

"THE TWO LEVELS OF LOVE!!"

"LOWER LOVE IS AN ATTACHMENT TO PEOPLE, THINGS, OR IDEAS. HIGHER LOVE HAS NO ATTACHMENTS. IT IS A GIVING WITHOUT EXPECTING ANYTHING IN RETURN."

two divisions; POSITIVE EMOTIONS, and NEGATIVE
EMOTIONS.

NEGATIVE EMOTIONS are the emotions of fear, hate,
anger, jealously, and envy. They are the emotions
that send out negative feelings and vibrations to
other people or to other things. The powers of
these negative emotions are very great and de-
structive. They can destroy the people or thing
that they are sent to, and they also destroy the
sender.

POSITIVE EMOTIONS are the emotions of love, hope,
and faith. These emotions are constructive and
building, (not tearing down). The emotion of love
is not only powerful for the person receiving
the love, but it is also powerful for those sending the love, (you get what you give).

Think for a moment of the different negative emotions, and how powerful they are. Think about
FEAR. Fear is a negative emotion that eats within us. We are afraid that something terrible is
going to happen to us or to someone else. There
is always an object of our fear. We are afraid
for someone or something. We're afraid our car
will be in an accident, or that we will lose our
job.

The power of this negative emotion, fear, is very
great. Fear holds us back, and love frees us.
Love takes us forward. Love and fear cannot live
together at the same time, nor can a positive
emotion and a negative emotion be present at the
same time. However, you can have several negative
emotions at the same time, as can there be several
positive emotions together.

In the Bible, John I, 4-18, we find, "There is no
fear in love; but perfect love casteth out fear,
because fear hath torment. He that feareth is

not made perfect in Love". It further says, "We
love Him because He first loved us. If a man say
I love God and hateth his brother, he is a liar,
for he that loveth not his brother whom he hath
seen, how can he love God whom he hath not seen?"
"And this commandment have we from Him, that he
who loveth God, love his brother also."

What the Bible is trying to get across to us is,
that we should get rid of our negative emotions,
and replace them with positive emotions, with
love and faith.

Emotions are the prime movers, the directors and
the carriers of our thoughts. We can send our
emotions in whatever direction that our thoughts
may turn. If we have strong emotions about a person or an object, then these strong emotions would
be the carriers of the vibrations that go out to
that person or object. If we are concerned about
another's well being, and our concern is out of
unselfish love, then this emotion of higher love
would be like sending out a prayer of protection
to that person. It would surround them with our
love and help and protect them.

The powers of love can be many. There is nothing
that our unselfish love cannot do. It is one of
the highest things that we can give to another,
and it is also one of the best things that we can
do for ourselves.

ALL OF THIS INFORMATION IS JUST SO MUCH USELESS
KNOWLEDGE IF WE DON'T APPLY IT, AND USE IT IN OUR
OWN LIVES. FOR TRULY THIS IS WHERE WE CAN DO THE
MOST GOOD FOR MANKIND. TO WORK ON OURSELVES AND
TO GET OUR OWN LIVES IN ORDER.

"YOU REAP WHAT YOU SOW!!"

"WHEN YOU SOW LOVE FOR YOUR FELLOW MAN, YOU WILL REAP LOVE."

WHO REALLY WAS THE SON OF GOD?

Since time began, the world has had great enlightened beings such as CHRIST, BUDDHA, and KRISHNA.
Who were these beings, and how were they able to
do the things that they did? Were they the sons
of God?

Quoting from the Bible, Matthew, 16-13. "When
Jesus came into the coast of Caesarea, Philippi,
He asked His Disciples saying, 'Whom do men say
that I, the son of man am?' And they said, 'Some
say that thou are John the Baptist, some Elias
and others Jeremiah, or one of the prophets'. He
sayeth unto them, 'But whom say ye that I am?'
And Simon Peter answered and said, 'Thou art the
Christ, the Son of the living God.' And Jesus answered and said unto him, 'Blessed art thou Simon
Barjona, for flesh and blood hath not revealed it
unto thee, but my Father which is in Heaven'.
Then charged He His disciples that they should
tell no man that He was Jesus the Christ."

Jesus never referred to Himself as the Son of God,
or as God, He always referred to Himself as the
Son of Man. And in this chapter of the Bible, it
shows that He told his disciples not to tell anyone that He was Jesus the Christ, or that He was
the Son of God. All throughout the Bible He continually told people to worship their Father in
Heaven and not Him. He continually referred to
Himself as the son of man.

The word Christ comes from the Greek word CHRISTOS,
meaning, Anointed one, or Blessed one. The
Christos sprit was in Jesus the man. "I and the
Father are one," said Jesus. Our Father in Heaven
is within us just as He was within Jesus. It was
Peter who declared that Jesus was the son of the
Living God. THE LIVING GOD. For God lives within
all of us, and all of us are the sons of the

Living God. No one can reveal the true meaning
of this to us, and when we truly understand this,
it is because it has been revealed to us by our
Father in Heaven, (our higher self) as it was to
Peter.

Over the past two thousand years, the Bible has
been translated, revised, and re-translated many
times. Much of its true meaning has been lost in
these translations. Some words changed and some
words could not be translated to have the meaning
of the original language. Many of our cultures
today have their own language meanings. Different
cultural words, when translated into another
language, have a totally different meaning.
Imagine how it would be to translate into another
language, our slang term, "Your mother wears com-
bat boots". Can you imagine the frustration and
misunderstanding of that statement if it were
translated into Russian or any other language?
They would not understand the true meaning of it.
And so it is with many translations and revisions
of the Bible.

There have been, in the history of the world,
many other stories that have the same theme as
the story of Jesus' life. For instance, in some
ancient religions, the son of God was either the
son of a virgin or of some miraculous birth. In
India, the Gautama Buddha was born of a miraculous birth from his mother, Maya. In this birth,
his mother was overshadowed by the Holy Spirit,
and was advised that a holy child was to be born
to her. Angels also appeared to the father, a
king, telling him of the coming birth and telling
him how great a person his son was to become.
Upon the Buddha's birth, many angels and high-
beings came to earth and sang praises to him and
told of his greatness to all mankind. Many wisemen appeared telling the people how great the new
baby was.

As the Buddha grew up he, like Jesus, was tempted
in the wilderness by many demons and the devil,
which he overcame. He later in life became enlightened and set out upon his mission of spread-
ing the teachings to all mankind, as did Christ.

Another similar story to the birth of Jesus, was
the birth of Krishna, who was a high being in
ancient India. When Krishna was born, he also had
chorus' of angels saluting him and praising his
name. There also were wisemen coming to inform
the people of the high being that had just been
born. When he was a baby, he had an uncle who was
trying to kill him. This uncle, like Herod, order-
ed all newborn male children, in his domain,
slaughtered in hopes that he would slaughter Krishna and therefore prevent him from becoming a powerful king. There are many tales of Krishna's
fantastic powers of healing and of astounding his
teachers when he was a child.

In Persia, there was a great person born by the
name of Zoraster, who was said to have been born
of a virgin, in a cave, at midnight, on a date that
is approximately the same as our December 24th.
There are many books and sacred teachings of the
Zorathustera religion that teach that there also
was a bright star and celestial beings that sang
praises to the birth of Zoraster.

All of these great beings had the miraculous power to heal the sick and bring the dead back to
life. Another thing they had in common was their
belief and their teachings that they were not to
be worshiped as a god. They taught that they were
the son of man, and that God was within. It was
their followers who changed the teachings and added that these high beings were to be worshiped as
God. Today, the different religions worship these
men instead of worshiping the Father within, (which
is also the Father within us.)

Throughout the Universe there is only one life, one energy and one God. We are all a part of that one God. That one energy and that one life. Only our individual minds and bodies make us separate from each other and from that one God. Christ knew and all of those other high beings knew that we are a part of the living God, and the living God is within each and every one of us.

The teachings and the sacred writings of the Great Ones of the world have been written and passed down to their followers throughout the ages. Christ's disciples taught what they felt were the teachings of Christ, and Buddha's disciples taught what they felt were the teachings of Buddha. So it has been with all great beings and their followers throughout the world's history. As these disciples passed on, new followers would take their place. Each time the power would transfer from one man to another, a little of the teachings would be lost or changed. Throughout the centuries the original teachings have been so changed that the Great Ones would not recognize many of their own teachings if they were to see them today. It has been the followers who changed the teachings from what they were originally.

But this is not to mean that the great beings like Christ, Buddha, or Krishna will never come back to the Earth. Nor do I mean to imply that there have not been other great beings born on Earth. There have been many Christs and many Buddhas born. These are the enlightened people who, throughout the centuries, have come back to help mankind progress a little further on the path toward enlightenment. There are enlightened beings in physical bodies today. There are a few throughout the world, but you must discern them and find them for yourself. People today, as in Christ's day, do not recognize these beings.

They do not call themselves the Son of God, or a
God to be worshiped. They refer to themselves
merely as a son of man, as Christ did when he
walked the earth. But a word of caution. There
are also many false prophets on earth today. Be
very cautious in your dealings.

All of us are really sons of God. Each of us has
the ability to become enlightened as the Great
Ones were. As in their case, it took many lives
of hard work to reach that point. It was not easy
for them, and it will not be easy for us. We must
continually work on ourselves, following the path
that they have taken, and following the rules that
they have set down.

Christ said, "All that I do, you too can do, and
much more." He really meant it. We are the sons
of God, and can be enlightened as were the Great
Ones.

ALL OF THIS INFORMATION IS JUST SO MUCH USELESS
KNOWLEDGE IF WE DON'T APPLY IT AND USE IT IN OUR
OWN LIVES. FOR TRULY THIS IS WHERE WE CAN DO THE
MOST· GOOD FOR MANKIND, TO WORK ON OURSELVES AND TO
GET OUR OWN LIVES IN ORDER.

"WE ARE ALL THE SONS OF GOD, CONNECTED TO EACH OTHER. AND EACH OF US HAS THE ABILITY TO BECOME ENLIGHTENED AS THE GREAT ONES WERE."

XIV

WHAT IS THE PURPOSE OF MEDITATION?

The subject of meditation is quite often the most misunderstood subject, but yet the simplest practice we can do. It has been described by many people to mean many things and rightly so. Meditation _is_ many things.

It is like saying to somebody that you own an automobile, but it doesn't tell the person what kind of car you have. There are many types and styles of cars and so it is with meditation. There are many types, styles and methods of meditation for many different purposes.

Webster's Dictionary defines Meditat_ing_ as: "To think about constantly, to plan, intend, propose, to think deeply and continously, to reflect upon." It defines Meditat_ion_ as: "The act of meditating, deep continued thought, reflection or the solemn reflection on sacred matters, as a devotional act." A very simple and concise definition for such a deep and complex act. But is it a deep and complex SUBJECT? No, I think not. I think that it is a simple subject, and a simple procedure for doing something that will benefit you greatly. In fact, that is the reason for so much confusion about meditation. Many think that it must be more difficult than it really is.

Most people, born in the United States, have been raised into some type of religious teachings. And, therefore, are quite used to the habits and practices of prayer. The word prayer has many meanings, varying with the spiritual development of each individual. I once heard a good comparison of prayer and meditation. It was said that prayer is our talking to God, and meditation is our listening while God does the talking. There is another definition of meditation that I like and it is, "The liberation of the mind from all disturbing and distracting emotions, thoughts and desires".

I think meditation can be divided into two groups,
NON-DEVOTIONAL MEDITATION and DEVOTIONAL MEDITAT-
ION. The non-devotional meditations are the ones
that we do when we are alone. When we are just
sitting, relaxed and thinking about one specific
subject. Or when we are driving the car and all
of a sudden we discover that we are at our destination, but we don't remember getting there.
It was because our minds were in a meditating
state. We were meditating on a subject, and the
reflexes and actions of our body were natural and
automatic. Our car was driven to the destination
without our even thinking about it. It is this
non-devotional meditation that Webster's Dictionary is defining for us.

DEVOTIONAL MEDITATION must, therefore, be upon a
religious or high truth type of teaching, or subject. With this type of meditation we come the
closest to our Father in Heaven. Devotional meditation has several steps which must be followed
to achieve the best results:

    1. RIGHT INNER MOTIVES FOR MEDITATION.
    2. RIGHT ATMOSPHERE FOR MEDITATION.
    3. PROPER POSTURE.
    4. CONCENTRATION.
    5. PURPOSE OF THE MEDITATION.

Since a non-devotional meditation can be done
anywhere, anytime and on any subject, I will,
therefore, try to describe all of the points and
procedures for a DEVOTIONAL MEDITATION.

1. There is only one RIGHT MOTIVE for mind development meditation. It is an understanding of the
nature and the purpose of man's evolution. And
with this understanding there is a definite desire
to hasten that evolution in order that all life

around us may be the sooner brought into enlightenment or become one with the Father. With this motive in the back of our mind, our lives become a lot less complicated and easier to live. "Know thyself", said the Delphic Oracle. The way of meditation is the way of knowledge and the aim of all such knowledge is to find and to identify ourself with the self within, (our higher self). It is, therefore, of extreme importance to possess some knowledge of the nature of our Father in Heaven, in order that the purpose and techniques of meditation may be more fully understood.

2. RIGHT ATMOSPHERE: It is very important that our surroundings and our mind be of the right atmosphere for us to meditate. (Later on, as we become more accomplished meditators, this is not so important.) We will find that we can meditate anywhere and at any time. Even as some Hindu Indians have been able to meditate on piles of garbage in India. But for me, I would rather meditate in a nice, quiet, sweet smelling surrounding.

If your surroundings are comfortable, warm, well ventilated and plesant smelling. If they are familiar and of the quality and vibration to relax you, and give you peace of mind, then your meditations will be much easier. The beginning meditator will find it very difficult to sit down in the factory next to a vibrating machine and try to meditate. It is very important to have a quiet place to meditate. In meditation, we try to achieve a one-pointedness of the mind. If there are many outside distractions, this would be very difficult.

Your right frame of mind is also very important. If you have just had a fight with your wife, or husband, and then go in to meditate, it won't come easy. All you will be able to think of is that fight that you just had. If you are very anxious about something, that also will consume your mind. It is so necessary to have peace and quiet within yourself for a good meditation.

3. PROPER POSTURE: Relaxation and concentration are very much intertwined. We cannot concentrate when we're tense. The tension and restlessness in our body is a disturbance to our mind. One of the best ways to relieve this tenseness is a systematic relaxation of our body. This leads the mind towards concentration as it focuses on the various parts of our body.

Before we begin, we must assume a meditating posture which is steady and comfortable. And a posture such as this will insure that our head, neck and trunk are erect and in one straight line. Our back should be as if it were a tall stack of coins that had to be straight to keep from toppling over. The body should be made absolutely motionless. This brings our active senses under control. You will find that after you have meditated for awhile, that merely sitting motionless in a meditative posture will induce a feeling of relaxation and peace within you.

It is not necessary to sit on the floor or on a cushion in a lotus position. A person can meditate while sitting comfortably in a straight chair. But it is still important that the head, neck and trunk be erect and in a straight line.

After we are in this meditative posture, we should systematically relax each muscle and joint in our body thoroughly and completely by concentration. this type of relaxation exercise has been used to cure migraine headaches and other such illnesses. Physical relaxation leads to calmness of the mind. Let the weight of the body sink into your seat. It may take at least five minutes to become relaxed.

It is very important to practice the relaxation until it becomes a habit with you. When the body is relaxed we can then quietly turn our mind and concentrate it on the subject we have chosen. Remember that concentration is not a matter of physical effort. To further help the body relax, several deep breaths should be taken. Breathing in and out, consciously watching your breath come and go at a steady pace, not eratic, but steady. (Following your breath also helps develop concentration.)

4. <u>CONCENTRATION</u>: Technically, concentration is the holding of the mind to a single idea, a one-pointedness at will. By using the will power. It involves freeing the mind from any association with desire and feelings and then focusing the mind quietly on a single thought. The will power is used upon the mind through the choice of impersonal objects for concentration. Objects that are without emotional associations.

It is true that most men learn to concentrate on worldly affairs and things that affect their daily lives. All of this concentration is directed towards the analysis, synthesis and comparison of facts and ideas, which lead the mind to stray from one thing to another. This type of concentration is very helpful, but the type of concentration that is needed in meditation is the power of one-pointedness of thought upon the subject at hand.

Concentration has neither ethical or spiritual value, and it doesn't call for any special time or place or posture for its practice. Concentration exercises are like those that a marksman would use in target practice, or that of a pianist in the practice of the scales on a piano. Only when the concentration of thought has been brought under control of the will power, can it be effectively developed for meditation.

One good thing about developing our concentration
for meditation and that is that we can do it at
any time of the day. We can concentrate our
total mind and thoughts on reading a book, on
breathing, or on any subject we choose, and at
any time. After we have learned to do it very
effectively and without great effort, then we can
achieve much in our meditation.

When a person first begins to concentrate, he is
faced with all sorts of distractions. Many people grow discouraged, feeling that they were
calmer before they started meditating. This feeling is only a result of our experiencing disturb-
ances that have always existed in our mind, but
which we were unaware of. These are the things
that are down deep within us, that we are suppres-
ing and not allowing to come to the surface.
When we meditate, we relax and release our ten-
sions, and allow these suppressed feelings or
emotions to come to the surface of our mind.
The things that have bothered us and irritated us
in the past, rise to the surface of our mind,
where we can see them. These are the things that
upset us or discourage us, (and it is also one of
the reasons for meditation.)

All of these things that have bothered us down
deep, can now rise to the surface where we can
work on them and get rid of them. It's like seeing, for the first time, all of the dust that has
been swept under the rug. It is only a stage of
change, so don't let it continue to bother you.
Keep working with it and eventually it will all
be gone, and you'll have much easier meditations,
free of discouraging feelings.

The following is a good sequence for the beginning of any period of concentration. The object
upon which one is to concentrate is first determined. Then you should clearly say to yourself,

"For the next few moments, I am going to concern
my mind with a single matter at hand, that of
learning to bring my thoughts under the control
of my higher self. For the purpose of bettering
myself, in order that I may do a better job of
helping others."

After this preparation is made, the mind is then
turned to the object chosen for meditation, and
should be kept upon it for the pre-determined
length of time. The object first used for concentration should be that which is entirely impersonal and objective. You should not use any
type of colors or anything that has an emotional
association. You should always be aware that
this exercise is devised for training in the use
of your will power, just as much as it is for the
studying of the behavior and patterns of your
thoughts.

Your mind does not want to be under control, it
wants to be a free thinker and do as it pleases.
That's why your mind, and body, jumps around like
a monkey when you try to concentrate on simple
things. Such things as becoming too hot, uncom-
fortable or hearing things in the background will
take your mind elsewhere. All sorts of things
will cause you to lose control of your mind. But
this should not happen, you should always gently
bring your mind back to one-pointed concentration
on your subject, whether it is a pencil or some
high spiritual ideal.

The results of one-pointed concentration will be
achieved more quickly if a person will practice
concentrating his attention on whatever he is
doing during the day. If he practices holding
his mind quietly and attentive to each little job
as it comes along. This deliberate paying attention to the job at hand helps to train oneself in
concentration. It will then bring quicker results

as well as stimulating self-awareness.

Concentration exercises are a re-education of
your mind so that it will become obedient to your
higher self, and will stop flittering from one
thing to another. True meditation begins when a
specific thought or idea can be allowed to lie
quietly in the mind. As this thought or idea
lies quietly in the mind, it's true nature is
then experienced.

5. <u>PURPOSE OF MEDITATION</u>: Here is where there
is a vast difference of opinion on meditation.
The purposes of the meditation are many and
varied. Just as in our example of the car, all
cars are good, however, a person drives a particular make and model because this is what
pleases him. So it is with the purpose of meditation. We do the type of meditation that
pleases us and that we feel the most comfortable
with.

If we were to meditate on a pencil, a word or on
anything else of this type, then we would be doing
a NON-DEVOTIONAL MEDITATION. In other words, we
are practicing concentration. And this in itself
is extremely important so that our concentration
be one-pointed. However, a DEVOTIONAL MEDITATION
must have a higher purpose.

There are many different types of meditations
taught throughout the world, and each one of them
is excellent. However, you must feel at ease
with, and compatable to that type of meditation
that you are doing for it to be the most beneficial to you. TM Meditation is now being taught
throughout the country. It is a meditation that
uses a sound vibration called a 'Mantra'. There
are also Zen Meditations, Healing Meditations, and
many other meditations for many different purposes.

You can go into almost any bookstore in the country, and find books on meditation. Each one of
them will say much of the same things and some
different things. The different things come under
this heading, (the purpose of meditation). So,
ask yourself the question, "what is my purpose of
meditation?", and "what do I want to achieve?".
Whatever your reasons may be, KNOW THEM, know
them completely and set out to accomplish them.

Each human life has two important aspects about it.
One of the first things is to strive to attain a
spiritual goal in life, and secondly, is to learn
to live in the world around us. Meditation actually works to help both of these. It should
never be used as an escape, under the pretext of
seeking higher enlightenment through solitude and
escape. Meditation should be accepted as a meth-
od of practice for our attainment of spiritual
union with our Father in Heaven. On the other
side of the coin, meditation can be used to help
us keep our cool, and live our worldly life to
its fullest.

Thus, the purpose of meditation is at least two-
fold. It is used to awaken the intuitive activities in our mental life, helping us to express a
closeness to our Father in Heaven. At the same
time it cultivates qualities within us, that help
us to live a more relaxed life and be able to
handle stress situations around us. The change
in our mental habits may lead to an intuitive approach to all problems and the growth of insight
and peace can in time establish an open line of
communication between the waking consciousness
and our higher self.

6. CONTEMPLATION: Although I have not included
contemplation in my list of headings, I do feel
that it is important to know something about it.

Contemplation in meditation is the stage that one transcends all else and comes into union with our higher self, (our Father in Heaven). There is very little that can be written about this stage of meditation, for its main objective is to carry our consciousness beyond the range of thought, and to leave it (or rise above it) to a unity with the One Life. Several Eastern teachings call this stage of experience SAMADHI. They define it as the conscious and complete absorption into the infinite, and that it takes place when the natural processes of our mind and body come to an end. It is the return of the power of pure consciousness to our essential form.

Contemplation is, also, an impersonal awareness of the essence of the thing that we are meditating about, and the way of reaching contemplation consists of achieving the utmost one-pointedness, of our thoughts, upon this given subject and then raising our conception of that subject at the same time as we raise our consciousness.

These have been the major points of Meditation, and when we boil all of this down, we come to the conclusion that Meditation has one major purpose and that is to help us. It does this either in the DEVOTIONAL MEDITATION by bringing us closer to our Father in Heaven, or in the NON-DEVOTIONAL MEDITATION by helping us to keep our act together and keeping peace of mind while we are working and living in the world today.

After each chapter, I have suggested that the information in that chapter is just so much useless knowledge if we don't apply it and use it in our daily lives. And this is the chapter that tells us how to use it. Meditation is the way to use the information, in this book, to improve ourselves. It is a way for us to work on ourselves and to get our own lives straight.

CONCLUSION

There are no conclusions to this book. There are only ideas, thoughts, concepts and challenges for the future.

I'm not an enlightened being, nor am I a great teacher. I am just someone who has asked questions, and who has tried hard to find answers to these questions. In this way, by putting these same questions before you, maybe I have created in you, a challenge. Maybe I have created in you, new thoughts or new ideas that will lead you onto seeking further answers of your own.

My answers to these questions should not be taken as the gospel, my answers are for me, and as I stated in the beginning, it is most likely that my answers will change. So, it is good that you should disagree with my answers. You should challenge them, and mull them over in your mind. Because when you disagree, when you have friction going on in your own mind, then you will have growth. THERE IS NO GROWTH WITHOUT FRICTION. The writing of this book has given me much mental friction, and hopefully a little more growth.

Therefore, dear reader, this is why I say, there are no CONCLUSIONS in this book, there are just hopes for tomorrow, hopes for finding new truths and new understandings. And if I have caused you to stretch a little further, dig a little deeper, or to think a little stronger on any of these subjects, then I have satisfied my goal and my purpose for writing this book.

MAY YOU ALL WALK IN PEACE, LIGHT, AND LOVE.

CONRAD GEORGE

"WITHOUT FRICTION
THERE IS NO
GROWTH!!"

"WHEN THINGS COME EASY, THERE IS NO CHALLENGE,
AND THEREFORE, NO ACCOMPLISHMENTS."